HOW TO OPEN AND OPERATE
A HOME-BASED
DAY-CARE BUSINESS

HOW TO OPEN AND OPERATE
A HOME-BASED
DAY-CARE BUSINESS

An Unabridged Guide

by Shari Steelsmith

The
Globe
Pequot
Press

Old Saybrook, Connecticut

Dedicated to my husband, Jim Duffin

Library of Congress Cataloging-in-Publication Data

Steelsmith, Shari.
  How to open and operate a home-based day-care business : an unabridged guide / Shari Steelsmith. — 1st ed.
     p.   cm.
  Includes index.
  ISBN 1-56440-486-2
  1. Day-care centers—United States—Handbooks, manuals, etc. 2. New business enterprises—United States—Handbooks, manuals, etc. 3. Family day care—United States—Handbooks, manuals, etc.
  I. Title.
  HV854.S72 1994
  362.7'12'068—dc20   94-15645
                                                                         CIP

Manufactured in the United States of America
First Edition/Third Printing

Contents

Acknowledgments

Thanks to Karen Townsend and Charolyn Gould for specialized help with the manuscript and to all the dedicated family child care providers, particularly Deborah Eaton and Camille Vandermeulen, who contributed to this book.

Introduction

For parents, finding good, reliable child care is often an ongoing struggle. Articles and studies appear routinely in the media describing the child care crisis working parents must confront. The good news for you is that this crisis provides a ready and waiting market for a family child care business.

If you are interested in learning how to provide a warm, safe, and stimulating environment for children and how to become a child care professional, all from your own home, then read on. This book will tell you explicitly what a family child care business is and how to open and operate one from your home.

1

Family Child Care—Is It for Me?

The Benefits of Family Child Care

There are many rewards in family child care. The principal attractions for most providers are three-fold:

Being at Home with Your Kids
These are the days of double-income families. It is economically necessary for most families to bring in two salaries. This usually means that the children are placed in child care while Mom and Dad go to work. Running a family child care means one parent has the opportunity to be at home with the children.

Increased Income
Staying home is all well and good, but it's nice to have food on the table, heat, and a mortgage company who likes you because you send the check in on time every month. Running a family child care is a stable source of income and can often be quite profitable.

Being Your Own Boss
There are many benefits in owning your own business. The flexibility and control that come with being your own boss are high on the list. You can structure your work hours, enrollment, and fees in ways that work best for you.

Hmmm, sounds great, you say. But is this really for *me*?

Is This for Me?

Family child care is a wonderful option for many of us, but not *all* of us. It behooves you to look carefully at your life situation, family needs, career goals, skills, and talents before making your decision. You may love and adore your own two-year-old but be ready to check yourself into a sanitarium at the end of a day with three two-year-olds underfoot.

There are many factors to consider when you are evaluating your own suitability for running a family child care business. Perhaps the first and most important is asking yourself, *Do I like being with kids?*

It seems an obvious question, but it's a critical one. Almost all of us love our own children very much and want to be with them. But not all of us like being with other people's children. This is not a character failing, but it is an indication that family child care is not for you.

Claire, a provider from Seattle, shared her thoughts on this matter.

> My good friend Lisa thought she might like to start a family child care. She had seen my success with the business, had a three-year-old son, and with a newborn daughter wanted to give up her part-time job and stay home with her kids. She asked me if I'd write her a recommendation for the licensing people. I had reservations right from the start. Lisa is creative and energetic with her kids, but she's not a very patient person. I'd seen her lose her temper in stressful situations involving more than one child. I told her frankly that her strength

lay in one-on-one interaction with children and I didn't think she would be happy dealing with three or more kids at once.

You will be happier and the children in your care will be happier if you truly enjoy caring for and guiding young children. Fortunately, most family child care providers do. If you are the right person to run a family child care, you are probably the "Kool-Aid Mom" in your neighborhood; children are naturally attracted to play at your house. Your own children are sociable and like to have other youngsters around to play with. You do so much substitute-parenting that you've begun to think, "I should get paid for this." By reading this book, you're well on your way.

Kinds of Family Child Care Providers

There are as many different kinds of providers as there are families. Here are a few common provider profiles.

- *The mom who wants to stay home with her own children and still contribute significantly to the family income.* This describes the classic and most common type of provider. Many of us are happiest when we can be with and available to our young children throughout the day. Some of us have special-needs kids who do better with a parent around than a caregiver. Running a family child care business is often the perfect way to meet the two objectives of being available to one's own children and adding money to the family budget.
- *The child care professional looking for more control and independence in her work.* Many providers start out working for centers, preschools, or even therapeutic day-care centers, which are designed specifically for children with special needs. Perhaps they disagree with the director's philosophy or would like the freedom to experiment with new kinds of activities. Sometimes they just need to earn more money! The bright lights of owning their own business beckon, and before they know it, family child care is their new career.

- *The single parent who finds that family child care is a wonderful way to earn a living while enabling her to stay home with her children.* When families separate, it is stressful and difficult for all involved. Children are asked to make a lot of adjustments: the loss of one parent; often a new home, school, and community; and almost always, a formerly at-home parent going out to work. Many single parents find it a blessing to be able to stay home and be more available to their children during this time.
- *The husband-and-wife provider team.* In today's economy, jobs are less secure and the idea of being in business for oneself is more and more attractive. There are multiple benefits to such arrangements, which are becoming very popular. You can apply for the larger license (for twelve rather than six kids) and thereby increase your income proportionately. Children benefit from having *both* a female and male caregiver. When you function as a team, the burdens of the business are shared. There are obvious hurdles to get over when you work with a family member, perhaps more so when partners live and work together in the same place, but husband-and-wife teams can be very successful and profitable.

How Is a Family Child Care Different from Other Kinds of Care?

There are as many styles of family child care arrangements as there are families. Each one has its own features unique to the provider who runs it. There are, however, some basic similarities and distinctions that make family child care different from child care centers, preschools, and a babysitter's home.

Each state defines family child care somewhat differently. In general, a *family child care* is a licensed and registered professional child care program in the provider's home, where children are cared for less than twenty-four hours a day. It is run by a provider who has some training in child development and early childhood education; this training can be obtained through previous job experience, academic degrees, or continuing adult education and professional seminars. The number of children cared for in the program ranges from one to twelve, depending on the license held. The age mix of the children is determined by the provider. There is usually a daily schedule of activities.

A *child care (or day-care) center*, meanwhile, is a local business or a chain (such as KinderCare) that cares for children outside the home in a center setting. These centers are also licensed, regulated, and must meet certain standards set by the state. Children are usually separated by age group and there can be as many as sixty or more children in one center, depending on the license held. There may, or may not, be a schedule of daily activities. Child care centers are usually in operation during normal business hours and employ a number of people. The director or manager usually has an early childhood development degree or background; many of the staff, however, do not.

A *preschool* is distinguished from both family child care and a child care center by its focus on education. The director and teachers commonly hold degrees in early childhood education (oftentimes advanced degrees). A formal curriculum based on current educational recommendations and the philosophy of the school is usually in place. In Montessori preschools, for example, the teachers are trained in the Montessori methods and implement them in the school.

A *babysitter*, whether it be your mother, nephew, or the teenage girl down the street, provides informal care for children. There is no set schedule or curriculum required for this kind of care. A babysitter can provide care on a one-time basis; on an as-needed basis; or on a regular, weekly basis (same hours each day). Caregiving can take place in the parents' home or in the babysitter's home.

Most people are not aware that many states have laws regulating babysitting. For example, in the state of California, you can care for children regularly in your home for pay, without a license, only if:

1. The children are your relatives.
2. You are watching only one family's children.
3. You are a parent participant in a babysitting co-op (no money changes hands).

Be very careful about caring for children in your home for pay without a license. If you break laws and someone turns you in, you could be fined or even receive a jail sentence.

A *nanny* is an employee of the parent; the parent is responsible for paying the nanny's salary and payroll taxes. She or he usually lives in the home and cares for the children. Nannies can, however, also work part-time and/or live outside the parents' home.

Another type of nanny is an "au pair," a student from another country who provides caregiving services in exchange for room and board and, usually, a living stipend. A nanny may or may not have training in early childhood education. Some nannies also have housekeeping responsibilities.

Keep in mind that family child cares, preschools, and child care centers are licensed businesses for which parents are not obliged to pay taxes, whereas legally, parents must pay taxes for regular caregivers in their own home.

Family child care, child care centers, preschools, babysitters, and nannies all serve an important purpose for children and parents. It would be a disservice to say that one is better than the other; quality child care can take place with any of these types of caregivers. It is important, however, to know the differences among them—especially if you intend to enter the stimulating, enjoyable, and profitable field of family child care.

Styles of Family Child Care

Since each home and provider is unique, every family child care is unique. Deborah, a provider for some ten years now, describes her child care.

> My background is in early childhood education. I worked for some time in preschools and then struck out on my own. I first opened a family child care for six children. Being a parent and a child care professional, I already had many materials. My background in child care convinced me to set up a cur-

riculum of activities. My child care runs very much like a preschool because it fits my philosophy and training.

As my business prospered, my husband and I decided to buy a new house. We had it built with an even larger child care in mind. I now have a special playroom that looks very much like a preschool, with cubbyholes for children's belongings, an art center, a block corner, and an outdoor play area.

Elaine, a new provider, has a different set up.

Our house really lent itself naturally to family child care. We have a large rec room with a small bathroom right off it. I have a look-through window from the kitchen so I can watch the children while I'm preparing lunch. The toys are all in the rec room and the children mostly stay there or we play outside in the yard. I'm a great believer in free play, so I don't structure the day much beyond meals, naps, and play time. I do make sure that all the toys and books are appropriate and learning-oriented. I didn't have money at first to provide highchairs and playpens, so I asked the parents of the two infants enrolled to provide their own. They were happy to do it.

And Laura, a former nurse, operates this way.

When I left nursing to stay home with my son, I knew many other nurses who worked swing shift or graveyard hours. I set up my family child care to accommodate the needs of these parents. I'm open from two o'clock in the afternoon until midnight. My husband works swing shift and I'm a night owl, so this works well for us.

As you can see by the above examples, there is no one standard family child care set-up—or one "right" way to run one. Each of these three women runs her business according to her skills, values, space, and availability. Your family child care will reflect your particular style. And the children will benefit from your background and experience. Now, let's start taking stock of your space and begin to think about how *your* business could be structured.

Do You Have the Room?

One of the first things to consider is your physical space. Most providers have some sort of living room/family room area they use for the main play room.

Is the room big enough for six kids? Twelve kids? Depending on the size of license you are applying for, you need to make sure you can accommodate all the small bodies and the toys that accompany them. One way to test this is to have six children over for a morning of play, followed by lunch. See how it goes. Are you tripping over each other? Do the children have room to spread out a bit? Are there conflicts over space? Remember that you need enough room for each child to stretch out on mats for a nap; you may choose to use bedrooms in the house for this, but many providers find it simpler to use the play room as a sleeping area as well.

Another issue is storage. Where will you put the children's changes of clothes, coats, boots, or other items brought from home?

Think about your bathroom—is it easily accessible to the play room? Children will need to get there quickly and with as little guidance from you as possible. If they have to trek down through a hall, around the corner, and up the stairs, you have a problem. Preferably, the bathroom will be right off the play room. If it isn't, think about how to make it more accessible to the children. Perhaps you could move your couch to another part of the room and clear a more direct path to the bathroom.

Some providers like to use a separate side or back entrance for the children and their parents. While this isn't necessary, some providers find that it helps keep their family and professional lives a bit more separate.

Consider your kitchen. Where will the children eat? Maybe you're incredibly blessed and bought a house with a low breakfast bar. Perhaps your mother had high hopes for a lot of grandchildren and she bought you six child-sized chairs for the bar. That's wonderful; you know where the children will eat. But maybe you're just an ordinary homeowner and you have a regular table with adult-sized chairs. Don't worry; you can still successfully feed the children. You just need a little flexibility and creativity.

One provider purchased two child-sized picnic tables and brings them into her kitchen at lunch time. The tables, each of which seats six preschoolers comfortably, do double duty as the site of art activities as well. Another provider had a woodworker relative build a few child-sized tables for her. Another brought discarded coffee tables into service.

Some adult-sized tables work admirably as they are. Some providers use booster seats or other safe ways to bring a child's nose up off the table. You can also invest in a few sturdy child-sized tables and chairs from any one of the numerous preschool supply company catalogs (see Appendix).

Let's go outside. Front yards are not usually workable for child care since they are rarely enclosed. Backyards are commonly fenced. Do not despair if your yard is unfenced and unlikely to become so; in most states it is legal for you to have children in an unfenced yard. However, you just have to be there 100 percent of the time the children are outside—no running in to answer the phone, turn off the oven timer, or attend to other matters. All the children must be outside with you if this is the case. Needless to say, fencing is highly desirable.

Do you have room for outdoor play equipment? Many providers already have a sandbox, slide, or swing set. Think about your trees and plants. We will cover safety requirements more completely later, but now is a good time to cast a critical eye over your flora and fauna. Which plants are poisonous? Do you have thorny bushes that could be dangerous? Which hazardous plants are you willing to do without, or to transplant to a safer spot?

The most common outdoor hazard is a swimming pool. If you've got one, then you have very specific regulations to meet. Drowning is high on the list of causes of death in young children, so pool regulations are strict. Limiting access to the pool is crucial. In most states, it must be adequately fenced with no door or window access from the house. Again, we'll go over this more in chapter 2 of this book, which covers safety and licensing. At this point, what you need to do is begin to add up which areas of your home are workable, and which areas are likely to need changes.

Now that you've taken a preliminary look at your space, the next step is to take stock of your skills and background.

Take Inventory of Your Skills and Experience

Do you know enough about child development and guidance?

Well, let's see. If you are a parent, your practical experience could fill three books! You may have had a course or two in school on child care and development. You read parenting books and magazines. Perhaps you've had professional child care experience.

Everyone has some kind of experience or background, but more to the point, we can *always* use more. However much you already know about children, there is more to learn. New information and research on young children appear all the time. Every child is different; you will have easygoing and challenging children in every group. The more skills and information you have, the better able you will be to care for and guide these children.

There are three principal areas in which you might consider further study: child development ("ages and stages"), curriculum activities, and guidance (discipline). Numerous other areas are also relevant: For example, nutrition and safety are very important and much training on these topics is also available to you.

Most providers start out with little experience in dealing with other parents. Many providers describe dealing with certain parents as remarkably similar to dealing with their preschoolers. Your style of communicating with parents will either ease the inevitable problems or exacerbate them. Getting extra preparation and training will pay you back a hundredfold. A regional family child care support/networking group (discussed in chapter 2) will be of invaluable help to you here.

Training is also a form of support for you. Learning about children's ages and stages and acquiring new skills for handling common (and not-so-common) problems will help you to be more confident and effective. And it will naturally benefit the children in your care.

The best place to start is exactly where you are. Take stock of what skills and background you already have, then decide where your gaps lie. Here is a list of possible areas for you to seek continuing education in. Check off those that you wish to explore further.

___ Infant and child first aid and CPR
___ Age-appropriate expectations for children
     from infancy to age six
___ Guidance techniques
___ Nutrition
___ Parent-provider relationships
___ Child abuse awareness
___ Professional development and community resources
___ Business practices
___ Children's health
___ Special needs/children with disabilities
___ Multicultural/anti-bias awareness
___ Curriculum and activity ideas
    ___ Art
    ___ Science and math
    ___ Cooking
    ___ Movement/dance
    ___ Music
    ___ Language
    ___ Personal safety
    ___ Dramatic play

Take advantage of any training programs available to you. You can check with the following resources:

- Your local child care Resource and Referral agency often sponsors training courses and special seminars.
- Your state licensing department can refer you to relevant programs or classes.

- Many community colleges and universities offer early child-hood classes, parent education seminars, and courses in their adult continuing education departments.
- The YWCA often offers courses in parenting and child guidance.
- Your regional Family Child Care Association Group routinely makes classes and training available to you.
- Many magazines offer up-to-date information. See Appendix for suggestions.
- Your local library (or bookstore) is a resource full of guidance and activity materials.

Begin now. Looking at course descriptions will help you identify where your gaps as well as your interests are. Taking a class is an excellent way to spend your time while you're waiting for your license. Start reading and studying and take advantage of training opportunities as they come along.

Continuing to educate yourself and update your knowledge as your business grows and prospers is highly recommended. Not only will it benefit you and the children, but it is a wonderful marketing tool as well. Parents will see that you take the care of their children seriously.

Are You Willing to Run and Maintain a Business?

Family child care is many things: child-centered, nurturing, rewarding. It is also a business—*your* business. As far as the IRS is concerned, you are self-employed. Being your own boss includes running the business in an orderly, professional fashion. This means keeping accurate and organized records, obtaining the necessary licenses to run a business in your state, city, and neighborhood, filing the appropriate business taxes at the right times, and maintaining contracts and agreements with parents.

Believe it or not, this is not all that hard. By reading this book you will start out with a good amount of information on generating enrollment, filing taxes, keeping records, and much,

much more. Chapters 3, 7, and 8 deal with specific business topics. And remember there have been many providers before you. Their experiences, mistakes, and successes are there for the asking. Talk to experienced providers or take workshops available to you. The important thing to ask yourself now is, am I willing to operate in a businesslike fashion? If the answer is yes, then reassure yourself that the how-to information awaits you.

Taking Family Members into Account

Okay, you've got the space, your background is solid, you're committed to running a business, and you're ready to pick up your phone and find out about getting your license.

But wait. What about those other people who live in your house? Your family is crucial to the success of your family child care. If your spouse and children do not support your business, you will be miserable. A business in the home affects all who live there. Your family must understand how the business will impact their space and their claim on your time and attention.

Your home is the place where you and your family relax, play, and learn. Now it will also be the place where you work for eight, ten, even twelve hours a day. And not only will you work there, you will bring in a collection of lively, noisy, and needy children. It can get pretty crowded.

Most providers report that it takes some adjustment, and often negotiation and compromise, but their partners are usually supportive of the business. Their children are a different matter, however.

When there's a family child care in the house, young children must share their space, toys, and *their parents,* sometimes before they are even developmentally capable of sharing. Some children adjust easily and like the other children around. Other children are not so easygoing, dislike change, and don't want to share their moms under any circumstances.

Think about how your spouse and children will react to a child care business in their home. Talk with them about how it will impact each member of the family. Describe as realistically as you can what will happen. Before going any further, you must have agreement in your family about your plan to open a family child care. Below are a few helpful guidelines to get a discussion started.

Worksheet—
Questions to Ask Yourself and Your Family

1. Before the family meeting, list each member of your family. After each name, write down which concerns he or she will probably have about a child care business in your home.
2. How might you address these concerns? Jot down a few ideas. Go over your self-generated list of concerns and possible solutions before you hold the family meeting. This will aid you in bringing up possible conflicts during the meeting and in brainstorming solutions to problems.
3. Hold the family meeting. Describe your plan for a family child care. Explain how it would work. Ask each family member to share his or her concerns. Describe the benefits for the family and outline sacrifices the family would have to make. A sample family chart might look like the one on page 15.
4. If the concerns you predicted for each member are not raised, check them out. For example, "Zach, having a family child care would mean that I couldn't drop everything and go to the park with you whenever you want. We would have to plan our trips to the park in advance. Are you willing to plan your special time with me?"
5. Brainstorm solutions or compromises for the predicted problems. Look for win-win solutions.

If your spouse and children have concerns for which they are not willing to negotiate, then you need to seriously reconsider your plans. Perhaps this isn't the best time to open a family child care—next year might be better, when your two-year-old will be three and more capable of sharing you. Maybe you have a spouse who just isn't comfortable with the idea of "other people" in the house. Perhaps your thirteen-year-old needs your after-school involvement in her life more than the extra money the business would bring in. Everyone's needs are important.

Family member	Benefits	Sacrifices
Andrea (Mom)	More money for family; able to stay home with Peter; career satisfaction; no more commuting; able to set hours	Less time for family during work hours; some after-hours work; more tired at end of day
John (Dad)	More money for family; knowledge that children will be cared for by parent; no conflicts with Andrea over time off from work	Sharing home with children in care & parents; wear and tear on house & yard; less family time in the evenings when Andrea does paperwork
Zach, age 6	Mom will be home when he gets home from school; more money for hobbies like soccer	Sharing mom with the other kids; having family room space invaded after school
Peter, age 3	Can stay home with mom instead of going into child care; his best friend would be in care with Andrea	Having to share his mom, space, and toys with the other kids

Even with your family's encouragement and support, there will be conflicts and problems. But when there's a basic agreement to have the business, these problems are usually solvable. Chapter 8 will look at a variety of solutions to common problems.

Outfitting a Family Child Care on a Budget

You are undoubtedly wondering how much setting up your child care will cost. The answer for most people is, "as little or as much as you can afford." One of the beauties of family child care is that you already have your workspace. In terms of furniture, the basics include a high chair, crib or playpen, infant seat/carrier, and child-size chairs or booster seats. Most preschoolers can easily adapt to the furniture you already own. Basic supplies include toys, books, sources of music, and activity supplies (paper, crayons, paint, child-sized scissors, glue, etc.). You might also need safety gates, outdoor playground items, or additional storage space (cupboards and shelves).

Start with what you have and slowly add to it. Shop at garage sales, flea markets, and second-hand stores. Tell your relatives and friends that you'll take their discarded toys and equipment off their hands. Many regional family child care groups and Resource and Referral agencies have toy lending libraries; you can check out items for a specified period. Remember also to patronize your local library for children's and guidance books. Don't be surprised if you're able to skip the major toy retailers altogether.

Do keep some safety information in mind as you buy supplies. All items should be clean, sturdy, and free of any lead-based paint. Safety regulations on some infant furniture, such as cribs, have changed recently. Older cribs do not meet current standards for the width of space between the bars; the new standard requires that slats be 2⅜ inches apart and that any crib cornerpost extend less than one-sixteenth inch above the headboard. Another piece of equipment to be wary of is the baby walker. Pediatricians do not recommend its use due to its involvement in a high incidence of accidents. Use your common sense when selecting items for your child care, and check with your pediatrician for advice on any other items you have safety questions about.

Ask your children which toys and books they are willing to donate to the business; be careful to explain that these items must be available to the children in care and cannot be monopolized by the original owner.

In the beginning, you may wish to ask parents to bring what you are lacking. One provider started out by *asking* the parents of infants to provide their own playpens and high chairs. One year later, she was fully equipped. Another provider makes it a *policy* for parents to bring their own playpens. You can do what works for you. But keep in mind that it usually creates problems when children bring their own toys; many feel possessive about special toys and are not willing to share them. Books and videos, however, are by nature things to be shared.

One provider says she began her first family child care with $100. When she moved into a new home and increased her license to twelve children, she spent more.

> We earmarked one particular room for child care as our new home was being built. After all was said and done, I spent about $1,000 in tables and chairs, mats for napping, outdoor play equipment, and some additional fencing to block the play area off from the rest of the yard.

The Three Most Common Reasons a Family Child Care Doesn't Succeed

Lots of people leap into family child care and leap back out just as fast. There are three common reasons why this happens.

Lack of Clear Policies

Janet, a mother of two preschoolers, decided to begin a family child care business to care for the children of working parents in her neighborhood. Because she knew these parents fairly well, she didn't see the need to have formal contracts and policies for pick-up and drop-off times, vacation times, and fees. Gradually, parents began to take advantage of their friendship with her and abuse the casual pick-up time of 6:00 P.M. Janet had set. Soon, Janet had children in her home up until 8:00 P.M. without prior notice. These children needed to eat, so Janet fed them dinner. Janet began to feel ill-used, but hesitated to say anything: Since there weren't any rules, the parents weren't really breaking any. Her profitability went down because she had no late fee policy and was forced to feed the children who were staying late.

Frustrated and worn out, she attempted to set some boundaries and establish fees for late pick-ups. Some parents felt insulted when her rather irritable announcement reached them and they took their children out of her care. Bad feelings in the neighborhood resulted. Janet decided that family child care just wasn't worth the hassle.

Lack of Support from Partner and/or Children

Lisa, a new provider, had been working for a child care center in her community for about six months. Displeased with the large number of children in her care, she decided that a family child care would allow her more opportunity for closer supervision and teaching of the children. Her husband, Tony, was dubious about the idea, but liked the fact that Lisa would be there when their second-grade son, Brian, arrived home from school; he consented to give it a try. Thinking that Brian would like having his mom home more, his parents didn't think to consult him.

Things were very difficult at first. Brian didn't like the children in care anywhere near his room or toys, and he clearly wanted to have his mom all to himself. Second grade was proving difficult for him and he often came home tense and grumpy. Lisa, busy with six active preschoolers, had little time to talk with him.

Instead of getting better over time, the situation worsened. Returning home from work, Tony found that the clutter of toys and racket of children leaving for the day got on his nerves more than he had anticipated. He disliked having his space disrupted during the time of day he most wanted peace and quiet. Tony and Brian gave Lisa an ultimatum: Either the child care had to go or they would!

Lack of Developmental Information on Children's Different Ages and Stages

Karen had always loved children. She babysat a lot growing up and had two children of her own, ages two and four. Family child care seemed a natural choice for her. Enthusiastic about the idea, she charged ahead, taking in four children in addition to her own two. She planned eventually to upgrade her license to take twelve children.

Soon, however, Karen found that the five two-year-olds and one four-year-old were chaotic at best and frequently unbearable. Since she didn't have a lot of capital to start with, she planned for the children in care to play with her own children's toys, or to bring their own. When there weren't two of one item, she expected the children to share or take turns. It didn't work that way at all. Karen found herself explaining over and over again why the children had to share and policing them when they didn't.

Worse still, many of the two-year-olds didn't separate easily from their parents and spent the first hour in her care crying. Mornings were particularly unpleasant this way. Karen worried that perhaps she was a bad provider if the children hated to come so much.

Feeling desperate and completely bewildered, Karen closed her child care.

The above scenarios can all be avoided. With adequate research, you can set clear and fair policies. With enough communication, you can determine if family child care is viable for your family members. With proper training, you can make good decisions about the age-mix of children and have realistic expectations of their abilities. The important thing is to think about these issues ahead of time.

Visit a Provider

One of the best ways to decide if family child care is for you is to visit an experienced provider (or two, or three). If you know someone, great, go see her. If not, ask around; a friend or family member will suggest someone. You can also call your local Child Care Resource and Referral agency for some names and numbers.

Providers are a busy but friendly lot. Most are quite happy to answer your questions and show you around. Observe the layout of space. How does the provider use the rooms and yard? Which rooms are off-limits? How does she deal with safety hazards, like pools or hot tubs? What things did she need to change to become licensed?

If you can, visit while the children are present. Notice their activity or level of focus. Do they run right up en masse to you because the toys and activities aren't engrossing enough? Or do they gradually notice you and come in smaller groups to greet you?

Ask the provider what her greatest challenges are in running a family child care. What is her background? What problems did she have in her first year?

Visiting providers before you open your business will help you to set up your own network of colleagues. Running a family child care can be isolating. Meeting and sharing with fellow providers will make your job easier and more enjoyable.

You've done a lot of thinking and taking stock in this first chapter. You've looked at what exactly family child care is and what the benefits are for you. You've taken inventory of your home and your skills. You've taken a good hard look at your family and begun to determine how well they would adjust to having a family child care in the home. And, you've thought about the business tasks and professionalism necessary for running a home-based business. If you believe family child care is for you, now it's time to move on to chapter 2 and act.

2
Starting Out

You've done your soul-searching and you're ready to start. Begin by contacting the National Association of Family Child Care and then move on to the licensing and registration process. Finally, sit down with a pencil and paper to estimate your monthly income and expenses.

Where to Start

The National Association for Family Child Care (NAFCC) is a professional association for home-based child care providers headquartered in Washington, D.C. (See Appendix for its address and phone number.)

Call and get information on joining now. Then, when you've received your license, join NAFCC. It is chock full of helpful information for beginning and experienced providers. A few of the services and resources it offers are:

- A bimonthly newsletter, *The New National Perspective*
- Accident and liability insurance information for most states
- Resource publications (available by mail order)

- National Family Child Care Conference (held biannually)
- Directory of regional Family Child Care Associations and support groups

As of Spring 1994, membership for an individual provider was only $20 (tax deductible as a business expense). For the amount of help, support, and referrals you get, this is a true bargain.

NAFCC is also quite active in advocacy and child care legislation on the national front. It is a powerful voice for children and for you. In addition, it has developed an accreditation program for providers who have been in business for eighteen months or more. We will talk more about accreditation in chapter 9.

Joining NAFCC will plug you into the most organized family child care network in the country. Your membership in NAFCC is also reassuring to parents who are seeking quality child care.

The Next Step: Licensing and/or Registration

Nearly every state requires providers to be either registered with or licensed by the state or county agency that regulates child care. This requirement means that you cannot care for children in your home without being appropriately licensed. If you are caught doing so, you can be fined for each day you operate without a license and can be jailed. To avoid this very unhappy turn of events, be sure to read this section carefully and be extra thorough in your research.

The licensing process generally begins with an orientation session (usually held at regular intervals at a central location in each county), continues with your written application and a visit from a home inspector, and concludes with your compliance with any changes the inspector asks you to make. It is a straightforward process, but one in which it is essential to pay attention to every detail.

A Word of Explanation and Caution

This is a very, very important point: *Not all states' requirements are the same.* What is true in Georgia or Colorado is not necessarily true in Minnesota or New York. Each state is free to set its own rules and each has done so. For example, nearly all states have strict safety rules; however, each of them has different specifications for how these rules are to be implemented. If your cousin who is a provider in New Hampshire can fence her pool at a certain height and meet safety regulations, it doesn't mean you can do the same in Florida. If your fire extinguisher meets the safety code in Idaho, it doesn't necessarily meet the code in Arizona. Going through the licensing, registration, or certification process will put specific information into your hands about your state's rules.

Also keep in mind that some states' regulations vary *within the state.* One provider in California assumed that because her provider friend in a neighboring county could add an extra child to her capacity, so could she. When the inspector made his annual visit, he informed her that the other county had a special pilot project being tested and the extra child allowance did not apply in her county. She was found in violation of her license and fined.

Here's the second most important point: *You are responsible for knowing what the regulations are in your state and locality and for complying with them.* The provider above was fined because it was her responsibility to know what her county allowed. She should have checked it out before accepting an extra child.

This book cannot possibly list every regulation in every state. What it does is cover some areas that most states have in common and give you a *general* picture of what to expect. The information in this chapter is not intended to be complete for any state or for you to use as a sole resource. Remember: *It is your responsibility to inform yourself of what your state and county require and to comply.* The best way to start this is by going through your state's licensing process and reading all the regulations you are given.

Why Do We Need Licensing and/or Registration?

Quite simply, to ensure that children are properly cared for and safe. We would all agree that this is important. Unfortunately, the honor system doesn't work in this arena; people have vastly differing ideas of what is safe or appropriate for children. So the government makes the rules and enforces them.

Don't be intimidated. Think of the licensing folks as your colleagues, not as some interfering governmental agency out to get you (believe me, they're much more flexible than the IRS). They are in the business of setting a stamp of approval on your business, and that is worth a great deal. Good child care is hard to find these days, and they know it. They want to give you a license just as much as you want one. It is their job to make sure you meet all the requirements and they will work with you to help you do so.

Going through the licensing process is an education in family child care in and of itself. You will be amazed at the amount of information about children and child care you will glean from the regulations, orientation meetings, and inspections. You will also be grateful for the many hazards and hassles that the licensing process will save you.

Jeri, a provider of eighteen months, had this to say.

> The licensing process helped me avoid many problems. I never dreamed I had so many potentially hazardous items in and around my house. I thought that because my back yard was fenced, I was ahead of the game. I discovered that many of my ornamental plants were poisonous, the lock on my gate needed to be self-closing, and that two sturdy five-year-olds could easily tip over my old swing set! It wasn't a lot of work to correct these things; I transplanted the plants to my side yard where the children were fenced off from them; I installed a self-closing lock on the gate; and we got rid of the old swing set, left over from when my three kids were little. All the day-care children have been safe as can be in my yard.

The licensing process also plugs you into a network of suppliers and resources that serve the provider community. Most licensing agencies will provide you with information about your local child care referral agencies, food programs, training opportunities, and provider support groups.

You will get access to this network right from the start. At a recent orientation meeting for new providers in Riverside County, California, for example, I received a packet of handouts that included the following:

- The state of California's Regulations for Family Child care Homes
- An application booklet (containing all the necessary forms for applying for a license)
- Brochures for three local food sponsors (for participating in the federal food program, page 40 in this chapter)
- An application to be listed with the local Resource and Referral agency
- A handout of sample provider-parent agreements and policies from the county office of education
- Descriptions of two training programs immediately available in my community
- Information on the local Resource and Referral agency with a description of services available

The director from the local Resource and Referral agency was also on hand to explain the agency's role in family child care and to answer any questions.

Whom Do I Contact to Get Licensed?

Look in the phone book. Call up the Department of Social Services (or whatever variation on the name your state has adopted) for your county or state. They will usually refer you to an office of community care licensing. Many such offices license and regulate not only family child care but also all kinds of child and adult care: foster care, child care centers, rest homes, state facilities for the disabled, and so forth.

The appropriate licensing agency will give you information on how and where to apply for a license, based on where you live. Generally, they will require you to attend an orientation meeting before you will be given the application forms.

If you're having trouble finding the licensing people (in these days of voice mail, it can be difficult to reach a live person instead of a recording), call up the National Association of Family Child Care (800-359-3817); they can direct you to the appropriate office in your state.

What If My State Has No Licensing Requirements?

If your state has no requirements, or has voluntary registration, there is good news and bad news. The good news is that you may not have to pay for a license and delay opening your business until you apply and are approved. The bad news is that your state has not yet recognized child care as a vitally important component in our society. This has repercussions both obvious and not-so-obvious. If child care is not regulated then children are not necessarily safe and well-cared for. If your neighbor down the street offers daycare for half the price you do, with twice the number of children and lets them sit in front of the TV all day, there's no legal recourse to the inequity or potential safety hazards.

It is in your best interests to follow the accreditation guidelines NAFCC has prepared for all providers (accreditation requirements are described in chapter 9). (Send for NAFCC's Code of Excellence for providers.) Just because your state hasn't gotten around to caring about the children who live in it, doesn't mean that you don't. NAFCC is active in lobbying for regulation in states such as Oregon, Louisiana, and New Jersey where licensing is only voluntary. Eventually, they will succeed in requiring licensing. Be prepared for this by meeting NAFCC's recommendations now.

NAFCC has ten regional representatives who cover all fifty states. Call yours up and ask her to refer you to the local support group in your area. The members of your support group can also give you advice and guidance for setting up your family child care.

The Basic Components of Licensing

The following information on licensing is not state-specific, but rather a general picture of what you will find when you read your regulations and go to your orientation meeting. It is your responsibility to find out about and comply with all your state's (and community's) specific requirements.

Size of License

You can get two kinds of licenses from the state: small (generally one to six children) or large (seven to twelve children). The maximum number of children cared for is usually referred to as your "capacity." In both cases, your own children ages ten and under count in your capacity. So if you are the mother of four children under the age of ten, and you have a small license, you are only allowed to take in two extra children.

If infants are cared for, your maximum capacity is further reduced. Check with your state for their definition of "infant" and their regulations regarding how many infants are allowed for large and small licenses.

There are additional requirements for having a large license:

- You must have evidence of at least fifteen units of early childhood education credits (a transcript will do), or one year of experience at a licensed child care facility, or be an experienced small family child care provider for at least one year.
- You must hire an assistant provider who will be present when the seventh child arrives. The assistant provider must generally be fourteen years of age or older. Many states also restrict providers from leaving the children alone with an assistant younger than eighteen years.
- You must have a legal business license and/or conditional use permit. (See pages 43 and 44 for more information on these kinds of permits and licenses.)
- After you have your business license, you must obtain an approved fire inspection from your local fire department or city inspector.

One last word on capacity is in order. If your children's friends come play at your house, they are considered part of your capacity if:

- They arrive without a parent present or at home available to them, and
- They are age nine or younger.

The BIG concern: Safety

Let's go on to the issue that's on everyone's mind: safety. You may be worried that expensive alterations will need to be made to your house or yard. This is probably not the case. Most providers find that a lot of minor changes need to be made, but the big ones (fencing a pool, removing a tree) are few and far between.

It helps to remember that all family child care homes need to be safe for the three age groups that they serve most: infants, toddlers, and preschoolers. What might not be a threat to a preschooler could be very dangerous to an infant—for instance, glass marbles at the base of a flower arrangement. What you'd trust a school-aged child with you would shudder to think about within a toddler's reach—for instance, easy access to the toaster oven.

One home inspector recommends that you get on your hands and knees and creep around your house. You'd be surprised at what you find down there. During her home inspection one prospective provider discovered that she had an uncovered air conditioning duct below her stairwell, big enough for a child to crawl into. The home inspector was not impressed.

Let's take a tour of *your* home.

Doors. Any door you normally keep locked but which you will need to use as an exit in case of emergency (typically the front door) needs to have a single-action lock. With this type of lock only one action is needed to unlock and open the door. For example, if you turn the knob, the door unlocks and opens at the same time.

While many providers like to keep the doors locked when everyone is inside, most inspectors feel it's more important to keep exit access open in case of fire or other emergency. Although locked doors can "keep bad people out," they can also trap fire victims inside. The state sees more instances of the latter, hence its prejudice toward unlocked doors.

Stairs. Young children (usually designated as under age five) are not allowed to go up and down stairs. If you have a stairwell, you must fence or barricade it.

Fireplaces. Fireplaces should have screens or doors to prevent any child access to them. Wood stoves should be screened or fenced in such a way that no access by children is possible. Open-face heaters should also be screened or placed in a room inaccessible to children. No inspector likes to see the old-fashioned style of bathroom heater with red coils. If you have one, prepare to replace it with something safer.

Fire extinguishers. Find out what your state requires. Often, the fire extinguisher required is larger than the size one usually has on hand at home. (Many providers recommend the "ABC" type of fire extinguisher that puts out all types of fires—electrical, paper, wood, etc.) Check to make sure that your fire extinguisher is easily accessible. If you usually store it in your garage, and your garage is locked while the day-care children are present, you have an access problem. Also, make sure that your smoke detectors are placed appropriately and have working batteries. States vary in how many and what kind of detectors they require.

If you are applying for a large license (seven to twelve children), or you are caring for children who cannot walk, then a fire safety inspection is generally required. Your local fire department or sometimes your city building department can do a fire inspection.

Poisons. Many, many substances are toxic if swallowed, spilled on skin or in eyes, or inhaled. Here are some general categories of items to beware of:

- Cleaning products—detergents, toilet bowl cleaners, disinfectants, furniture polish, and more
- Medicines—prescription drugs or over-the-counter medicines (such as aspirin, allergy pills, or salves)
- Other ordinary products found in your bathroom—rubbing

alcohol, shampoo, hairspray, or cosmetics
- Poisonous plants inside the home or outdoors
- Lead paint on walls, furniture, or other older items

There are hundreds more substances, commonly kept in homes, that are poisonous. When it comes to children, expect the worst. It is developmentally appropriate for young children to explore anything and everything, that's their job. It's your job to keep hazardous items out of their reach. Medicine looks like candy. Many cleaning products are a pretty blue liquid color, detergents can look like flour or sugar.

The point is to identify the harmful substances and *lock them up*. In fact, one experienced home inspector recommends that you take everything out of the bathroom the children will be using except toilet paper and soap. If this isn't possible, get locks for your cupboards and medicine cabinets.

Firearms. We all know that guns and children should be kept apart. If you have guns or other weapons in your home, they should be kept locked up in a gun locker, well away from children's access. Ammunition should be stored separately from firearms and locked up as well. Some states allow you to use trigger locks or remove the firing pins from guns. In no case should they be accessible to children.

Be very careful to read your state's regulations on guns. Some states even have laws against keeping a loaded gun in the house with your *own* children.

Utilities. Your home should be adequately heated and ventilated for safety and comfort. No space heaters are permitted. Gas heaters should be properly vented and permanently installed. Your home should also maintain uninterrupted phone, water, sewer, and garbage service.

Garages. There are some pretty dangerous things in garages, which is why the state isn't fond of letting children play in them. Lawn mowers, hot water tanks, freezers, insect sprays—all of these things qualify as hazardous to a small child. If you have remodeled your garage into a regular room, then the children may play there after your home inspection approves it. Don't let children into your garage unless you have specific license to do so from the state.

Bodies of water. This includes (but is not limited to) pools, spas, fish ponds, sunken wading pools, and hot tubs. Generally, the state requires that any body of water be fenced or covered with a cover that will support the weight of an adult. If the pool is fenced, then the pool area must not be directly accessible from a door or window of the house. It's not much use to fence a pool on three sides, just to have a child climb out a bedroom window and fall into the pool. Most states specify what kind of fence, and how high, is acceptable. There are also regulations concerning the gate to a pool.

Accidents are the leading cause of death of children ages one to fourteen and drowning is high on the list. There have been instances where young children drowned in buckets of mop water. You cannot be too careful about safety around water.

Backyard. Your backyard needs to be fenced according to your state's specifications, or you must be with the children every second they are outdoors. This means no running back in the house to get the phone, go to the bathroom, or anything else.

No toxic plants are allowed. Many common shrubs are poisonous, for example, oleander and rhododendrons. Call your local Poison Control center and ask for a list of poisonous plants. No dangerous plants are allowed either—for example, cactus or other thorny, spiky plants children could fall into.

Could the children tip over your swing set? All play equipment must be firmly installed and safe for rambunctious youngsters.

An unused refrigerator or freezer can be fatal if a child shuts himself or another inside. Any such unused appliances need to be strapped shut (or the door removed) and kept well out of children's access.

Pets. Many households have pets. How safe will the children and your pet be together? As one state inspector put it, "Everybody always says, 'My dog loves kids.' It isn't true. Young children are cruel to animals. Your dog does not love kids, he loves you; he merely tolerates kids. Sooner or later he will get fed up with being poked and prodded and will snap at a child."

Most states require you to keep your pets away from the children at all times, and vaccinate your dogs and cats for rabies.

In addition, no kitty litter boxes are allowed within children's access. Cat urine and feces are toxic, and kids think the litter box is a sand box.

For other common pets, such as birds or hamsters, check with your licensing agency. Exotic pets, such as alligators or Bengal tigers, are obviously not allowed.

Checklist. The following is a checklist of a few common problem areas for most prospective providers. Try answering the questions and checking out these areas in your home.

__ How safe are your houseplants? What would happen if a toddler ate one?

__ Are your bookcases secured to the walls? Could children (or an earthquake) tip them over?

__ Do you have cords or ties on any drapes or shower curtains? (Or anything else in the house that could choke a child?)

__ How overloaded are your outlets? Do you have safety plugs in unused electrical outlets?

__ Are your knives, and other sharp kitchen utensils, locked up, inaccessible to children?

__ Where do you keep your plastic bags? Could a child get to them and suffocate?

__ Do you have any oscillating fans accessible to children?

__ Are the toys and play materials in your home safe for the age group they are accessible to?

__ Do you have any flaking paint in your house? Have you had it tested for lead?

First aid. Most states require you to have some knowledge of first aid and CPR (cardiopulmonary resuscitation). NAFCC also recommends that providers be up-to-date in their first aid training. Classes and seminars on these skills are widely available. When choosing a class or seminar, make sure it covers first aid and CPR for infants and children (techniques for CPR and helping a choking child differ from methods you use on adults). Check with your local Research and Referral agency, family child care support group, or local hospital.

In addition, it's a good idea to have a first aid reference book around. Two good ones for adults are *A Sigh of Relief: The First*

Aid Handbook for Childhood Emergencies, by Martin Green (Bantam Books, 1979), and *Barron's First Aid for Kids*, by Gary R. Fleisher, M.D. (Barrons Educational Series, 1987). *Barron's* is in a chart format that is easy to keep handy and use. Another first aid reference, geared specifically to children ages four and up, is *Kids to the Rescue! First Aid Techniques for Kids* by Maribeth and Darwin Boelts (Parenting Press, 1992). This book is fun and educational for children, who love to practice and role play first aid. Lastly, make sure that all emergency numbers—Poison Control, Physician, Hospital, Fire, and Police—are posted near your phone for quick use.

Sick kids. In the interests of controlling infection, you are obliged by most states to separate a child who seems to be sick from the other children until he or she is diagnosed. If the illness is communicable, then the child must be kept separate from the rest of the group until the infectious stage is over. Most providers (unless they specifically service ill children) send sick children home until they are better.

TB test. Most states require all providers and their assistants (teen and adult) to have a TB (tuberculosis) test. Your family doctor or local health clinic can easily give you this test and a certificate. Your test must turn out negative and have been administered within the past twelve months. Your own children age fourteen or older, who are *not* acting as assistants, do not have to be tested. You will have to repeat the TB test every three years.

Emergency information. Generally, the state requires you to have on file specific information for each child in the event of an accident, illness, or other emergency. You should have, written down and easily accessible, the following information on each child:

- Full name.
- Date of birth.
- Phone number and whereabouts of parent (and at least one [maybe two] other responsible adult[s]) during care hours.
- Name and phone number of the child's physician.
- Authorization form granting you permission to obtain emergency care for the child.
- Allergies the child has.
- Immunizations the child has received.
- Any pertinent medical history on the child (past surgeries or illnesses).

A sample form showing this information is provided on pages 36–37.

Disaster plan. A disaster plan helps you, any assistants you have hired, and the children be prepared for emergency circumstances—for example, a fire or earthquake. You need to plan for such an emergency and practice with the children how they can safely exit the house. You'll need to draw up a floor plan that

Medical Consent Form

Name: Jonathan Andrew London

Date of birth: 10–1–90

Mother: Sue London
Work phone: 678-0936
Compton Electronics
5564 86th Ave East
Riverton, CT
Home phone: 677–7623

Father: Bill London
Work phone: 677–4746
Montgomery & Fitzgerald Assoc.
8562 Maple St., #250
Riverton, CT
Home phone: 677–7623

Physician: Dr. Elton, 677–8754

Immunizations: As of 12–1–93, up-to-date on DTP, Polio, MMR, Hepatitis B, Haemophilus.

Special information: Had episode with possible hernia when he was 12 mos old; allergic to cats.

Authorization: *Sally Sue Provider* has my permission to obtain emergency medical treatment for my child (including administration of anesthesia if a physician advises surgery) when I cannot be reached or if a delay in my reaching my child would be dangerous for him/her.

_____

Parent or Guardian

_____

Date

Authorization for Another to
Consent to Treatment of Child

Dear Parent:

This form may be used in the event that your child requires medical attention and you cannot be contacted. Please have the authorized person try to **CONTACT THE CHILD'S PHYSICIAN FIRST.**

If the physician cannot be reached, or if the physician feels the child should be treated in an Emergency Room, please bring this completed form with the child.

I, _____, certify that I am the Parent/Legal Guardian of the following children:

_____

Names and dates of birth

As such, I hereby authorize _____ of _____

Name   Address

_____,

Phone number

who is 18 years of age or older, to consent to any normal and/or emergency medical and/or surgical treatment of the above children that the above-named person deems advisable if I cannot reasonably be located through the information set out below when the children are brought in for treatment.

The above authorization will be effective as of _____, and will expire after six (6) months, or on _____, whichever occurs first. During this period the Parent or Legal Guardian of the above children will be at the following location(s):

Witnessed by: _____

Home address of Parent or Guardian: _____

Phone number of Parent or Guardian: _____

Employer: _____   Phone number: _____

Child's Physician: _____   Health Insurance Co.: _____

Phone number: _____   Group number: _____

24-hour number: _____

Child's Name	Chronic Illnesses	Allergies	Current Medications	Date of Last Tetanus Immunization	Other

shows an emergency evacuation plan (see sample below). Your licensing agency can guide you through this type of planning.

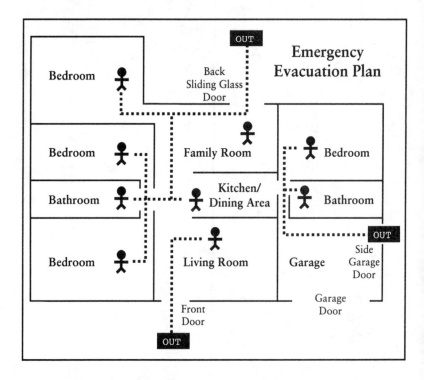

Criminal Record Check. It can be a bit daunting to realize that in order to work with young children in this country you have to be checked out by the FBI. Relax. You're a safe person, and you want everyone to know it. The purpose of this requirement is to keep children safe from those who would abuse or neglect them. All child care workers—from preschool teachers to camp counselors—are screened in some way, either by fingerprinting, a background check, or both.

The state isn't interested in your minor traffic violations, only in any *criminal* offenses on your record. Most likely the only "traffic" violations they would be interested in would be any driving while under the influence of alcohol, or if you've injured or killed someone with your car.

Licenses are routinely denied for applicants who have committed or attempted murder, done great bodily injury to another, committed voluntary manslaughter, rape, child molestation, pornography (or other sexually-related crimes), or who have had three or more drunk-driving arrests within the past year.

Crimes such as assault and battery and drug-related offenses are evaluated on a case-by-case basis, depending on the state's policy.

Obviously, there are a host of other crimes not mentioned here. If you are in any doubt as to their relevance to your application and license, disclose them. Honesty is critical here. If you lie about *anything,* your license will automatically be denied. It is not unheard of for the state to license a provider who is a recovering alcoholic or a recovering substance abuser; there may simply be restrictions placed upon her for driving with children in her care. So, if in doubt, tell the state about whatever unfortunate incident happened in your past and how your situation is different now.

The criminal record statement must be filed by you and any other adult who lives or spends a significant amount of time in your home. Your spouse, Grandpa who lives upstairs, your nineteen-year-old stepdaughter, your adult assistants, or Uncle Billy who stops by every Tuesday for coffee are all included. Be very careful how you determine "a significant amount of time." A good rule of thumb is to file for anyone to whom you give consistent access to your home (even if their appearances are irregular) during business hours. When your own children turn eighteen, you must file a criminal record statement for each of them within four days. In family child care, the majority of abuse cases that occur are committed by a family member of the provider: a spouse, grandparent, or teen.

Remember, you are responsible for the children's safety. If you allow someone to have access to the children and that person molests a child, then you can be prosecuted as an accessory to the crime.

Fingerprinting. Most states require fingerprinting. Usually, once your license application is accepted, the state will direct you to be fingerprinted so that your criminal record statement can be verified before the license is granted. Again, you must have all adults living in the home or spending a significant amount of time there fingerprinted. Your local police department, the motor vehicles department, and some notaries can fingerprint you. It can cost anywhere from $5 to $20 and is tax deductible as a business expense.

The record of your fingerprints will be added to the federal Child Abuse Index. This means that if you commit any crimes in the future, the information will be available via the Department of Social Services nationwide.

Car safety. Some providers regularly pick up children from school or other child care programs. If you do transport children in your car, there are some regulations you need to observe. First, and obviously, you have to be licensed to drive the vehicle in which you will be transporting the children. The car must be in safe operating condition. You should be fully insured. You cannot exceed the manufacturer's rated seating capacity for the vehicle; this basically means everyone has to wear a seat belt (no putting two children in one seat belt). Infants and toddlers must be in approved car seats (check your state's specifications for age and weight restrictions).

Although not required by the state, beefing up your car insurance coverage is highly recommended. The risks here are very great.

The topic of safety includes a myriad of issues, not all of which can be covered in one book. We've gone over some of the major areas the state is interested in. Read your state's regulations carefully for other, more specific safety requirements.

Nutrition and the USDA Child and Adult Care Food Program

Generally, the state doesn't have a lot to say about food, other than children shall be fed regularly and well. If children bring food into the house, it should be labeled with the child's name and properly stored or refrigerated; it should not be shared with other children. The federal government, however, has quite a bit to say about young children and nutrition.

Providers commonly take advantage of the U.S. Department

of Agriculture Child and Adult Care Food Program (CACFP) established by Congress in 1968. This program was originally limited to child care centers, but became available to family child care homes in 1975. It exists to improve the health and eating habits of children (ages twelve and under) by ensuring they receive nutritious, well-balanced meals while in child care.

What this means for you is you can purchase food from a licensed supplier and be reimbursed for a portion of the expense by the program. Many providers can thus supply all the meals children eat while in care for no, or little, extra charge. Parents like it because they are assured that their children are eating well and they do not have to take the time to prepare food to send with them each day. Face it, the children will eat your food anyway; you might as well be reimbursed for it.

Frankly speaking, it is cost-effective and smart to participate in this program. And it is relatively simple. Your local child care Resource and Referral agency can give you the name of your nearest food supplier. Your state can also refer you to suppliers. Call one of them up and make an appointment. A representative will call on you, explain how to use the program, how much money per child and per meal you will be reimbursed for, and how to keep appropriate records for reimbursement and for our old friends, the IRS.

The suppliers also provide other useful services. They offer workshops on nutrition, child development, creative menu and recipe ideas, and oftentimes they publish newsletters.

The crucial thing to remember when participating in this program is the importance of accurate record keeping. You must comply with the program's requirements for records or you will not be reimbursed. In addition, the IRS requires that you report the cash reimbursements as income; however, if you keep all grocery and food receipts, you may deduct the money you actually spend on food as a legitimate business expense. In the majority of cases, the money you end up spending exceeds the amount you were reimbursed by the program. We will go over the IRS requirements in more detail in chapter 7.

We will talk more about food when we discuss meal times in chapter 4.

Discipline

When it comes to guidance, or discipline, the state wants you to keep to the middle of the road. Most states are very specific about a child's personal rights. The following is taken from the state of California's rules and regulations for family child care homes.

> Each child . . . shall have certain rights which shall not be waived or abridged by the licensee regardless of parental consent or authorization . . . :
>
> • To be treated with dignity in his/her personal relationship with staff and other persons.
> • To receive safe, healthful, and comfortable accommodations, furnishings, and equipment . . .
> • To not be subjected to physical or unusual punishment, humiliation, mental abuse, or punitive interference with daily functions of living, such as eating, sleeping, or toileting.

There you have it, folks. No matter how much your patience is tried, *don't hit the kids.* We will go over several highly effective discipline techniques in chapter 6 that are generally approved of by early childhood educators.

Better Safe than Sorry: Liability Insurance

You either have to have liability insurance to cover possible injury to those in your home, or you have to have parents sign a statement stating that they are aware you do not carry it.

Warning: Your homeowner's insurance does not necessarily cover all the possible losses arising from family child care. You need to be protected from liability for bodily injury resulting from accidents on the premises, emergency medical expenses at the time of the accident, damage to someone else's property, and legal costs for defending against any suits.

Many providers carry special liability insurance for family child care as a "rider" to their existing homeowner's policy. You can find out more about this by contacting NAFCC or an insurance agency that specifically services family child care. Do this before contacting your homeowner's insurance company.

Frankly, it is quite dangerous to operate without insurance. Anyone can sue you at any time over anything, no matter how frivolous. Insurance premiums for family child care are tax deductible; don't risk your business and livelihood by skimping on this.

Inspections: How Many and When?

An officer or agent of the state will visit and inspect your home prior to licensing. The official will inspect your facility, discuss the record keeping required for each child, and inform you of any changes needed in your home and yard. The agent will give you an appropriate amount of time to make any needed changes before licensing.

After you are licensed, most states send out an agent once a year, unannounced, to make a spot check of your child care and ascertain that all is in order. In addition, if a complaint is made against you, the state will send an agent out to investigate, again unannounced.

The visits are always made during operating hours, and inspections are confined only to those areas the children have access to. If you are found in violation of any regulations, your license could be suspended or revoked and you could be fined. It all depends on the nature of the offense. If a portion of your fence blew down in the windstorm last week, you'll simply be required to replace it or keep the children inside. If, on the other hand, you're found to be exceeding the number of children you're licensed for, you will almost certainly have your license suspended and/or pay a fine.

City and Business Licenses

The state not only requires you to be appropriately licensed for family child care, it also wants you to be appropriately registered for business within your city. If you live within city limits, you need a business license. In addition, you need to be aware of local zoning laws. You may also need a conditional use permit to operate a business from your home.

This is important: *Find out about your zoning laws before you get too far into this.* Some residential areas, especially wealthy ones, are intentionally made difficult to run a business in. For example, operating a business from home may be legal, but will cost you an arm and a leg to get a conditional use permit. In these cases, it's obvious the city just doesn't want the perceived hassle of home-based businesses and is out to discourage you. If this is true in your area, contact your regional family child care support group for help and guidance.

If you are a lucky person, you live in an unincorporated area. Generally, city business licenses are not required in these neighborhoods. But the moral of the story is *find out.* Stephanie, a long-time provider, had this to say about business licenses:

> I used to live on the East Coast. The state and city had all sorts of licenses and requirements I had to meet. Then we moved to Salem, Oregon. Intending to set up another family child care, I called the city to find out what licenses I had to get. I said, "I'd like to start a business here in Salem." They essentially said, "So?" Their requirements were minimal compared to my previous state.

Planning to Make a Profit

A profitable business doesn't happen overnight and it generally doesn't happen at all unless you plan carefully. A simple calculation like the one on page 47 can help you figure out how many children you must take in and what fees you must set in order to be profitable. But first, you must make a detailed estimate of your expenses.

Start-up Expenses

Begin by listing your start-up expenses. By this time, you should have a good idea of what you already have and what you need. Here's an example:

Figuring Your Start-up Expenses *

Start-up Expenses

Fees

Child care license	$25.00
Business license	(Not applicable in my area)
Other necessary permits	None
Fingerprinting fee	$15.00
Child abuse index fee	$15.00
Fire inspection	$50.00
TB test	(Covered by health insurance)
Membership dues	$20.00
Other	None

Equipment

Fire extinguishers	$75.00
Fencing	None needed
Altering locks	$20.00
Outdoor play equipment	None needed

Furniture (small table & chairs)	$50.00
Other	None

Land Improvements

Repairs & maintenance	None needed

Supplies

Toys	$20.00
Books & tapes	$40.00
Activity supplies (art, science, etc.)	$25.00
Other	None

Office Expenses

Equipment (filing cabinet)	$25.00
Supplies (copies, file folders)	$15.00

Training & Education (R&R sponsored classes)	$15.00
Other	None
Total Start-up Costs	$410.00

*Note: Figures listed are for example purposes only.

Ongoing Expenses

Estimate your ongoing expenses by figuring out what they will be for one month. For expenses such as training, decide what you will budget for the year, and then divide by 12; that will yield a monthly expense for that category.

For food, figure your costs this way. Estimate how much you will spend on child care food for the month. At the time of this writing, the Child and Adult Care Food Program reimburses you per meal, per child on the following schedule: *

> Breakfast..............$0.8683
> Lunch...................$1.5208
> Snacks.................$0.4235
> Dinner.................$1.4525

*Note: These figures are subject to change. Check with your local food program supplier for current amounts.

Let's say you have six children in your care at any one time. You serve breakfast, lunch, and two snacks a day. If there are twenty-two days of child care in the month, then each child eats twenty-two breakfasts, twenty-two lunches, and forty-four snacks a month. This works out to the following amounts:

Reimbursement for 132 breakfasts (132 x 0.8683)   = $114.61
Reimbursement for 132 lunches (132 x 1.5208)   = $200.74
Reimbursement for 264 snacks (264 x 0.4235)   = $114.18

Total food reimbursement $429.53

Take your total estimate for food for the month, subtract the amount you are reimbursed, and you then have the amount you will actually spend on food.

See page 47 for how you might estimate your monthly costs.

Estimating Your Income

You can estimate your income easily. Simply multiply the number of children you plan to have by the monthly fee they will be charged. For example:

Number of full-time children.....5
Number of part-time children.....2
(Total capacity = 6 full-time children)

Monthly fee for full-time child:	$400.00
Monthly fee for part-time child:	$200.00
5 children x $400.00 per month =	$2,000.00
2 children x $200.00 per month =	$ 400.00
Total income per month =	$2,400.00

Figuring Your Ongoing Expenses *

Monthly, Ongoing Expenses	Cost per Month
Food (your cost after the food program reimburses you)	$215.50
Car Expenses	
Gas/mileage	$10.00
Additional insurance	$5.50
Liability Insurance	$35.00
Office Expenses	
Postage	$4.50
Membership dues	$4.25
Publications subscriptions	$4.25
Bank charges	$7.50
Laundry & Cleaning Supplies	$5.00
Other Household or Yard Items	$8.25
Repairs & Maintenance	$8.25
Supplies	
Toys, books & tapes	$8.50
Activity supplies (art, science, etc.)	$8.50
Other	
Training & Education	$20.75
Other	$15.50
Total Monthly Costs	$361.25

*Note: Figures listed are for example purposes only.

Profitability

Now that you've estimated both your expenses and your income, you're ready to determine if your business will be a profitable one.

Profitability Worksheet

Income per month:	$2,400.00
Expenses per month:	– $361.25
Net income (profit)	$2,038.75
* set aside for taxes:	– $611.51
Take-home pay:	$1,427.24

*You need to set aside a certain percentage of your earnings each month for federal and state taxes. Since the business expenses listed in the chart on page 47 are deductible, estimate the taxes on your net income. Your tax bracket is based on your total family income. Consult your accountant for a reasonable estimate. The above provider needs to set aside about 30 percent of her earnings.

According to this example, you can expect to earn about $1,400.00 a month after taxes. Of course, your tax bill may be even less than what is estimated here, depending on how diligent you are about record keeping in order to claim deductions. We will go over how to prepare for taxes in much more detail in chapter 7.

Keep in mind as you do this exercise on profitability that your actual expenses and income will vary from month to month. Your income will vary especially in the summer months, since both you and the children tend to go on vacation. This exercise is useful for helping you zero in on exactly how much money you need to bring in to pay the bills, pay yourself, and remain afloat. It also helps you keep your expenses in line with your budget. Once you open your business, you can do the books each month and get a good picture of your profitability.

It's Not Really as Hard as It Sounds

Licensing and registration can seem like a monster in governmental guise, but thousands of providers sail through the process each year. Know what you're responsible for and be careful to comply. You shouldn't have any undue trouble. Likewise, doing a realistic estimate of your expenses and income will start you off as a careful businessperson and help you get in the valuable habit of watching your cashflow.

In the following chapter we'll look at the next step in preparing to open your family child care: setting up your policies and procedures.

3

Policies and Procedures

One of the three top reasons a family child care business fails is lack of clear policies and agreements. Some providers get so swept away in the effort and enthusiasm of starting the business they forget to take some early, crucial steps. It is critical that you provide *written* policies and have parents *read and sign* them before you accept a child into your care.

After reading this chapter, you would do well to talk with any provider friends you have, and if you don't have any yet, to call up your local family child care support group for advice. Advice from experienced providers comes in handy when it comes time to set fees and policies. Ask questions, look at others' policies, and find out about the reasoning behind them.

Other good sources of sample policies and agreements are NAFCC, Redleaf Press (see Appendix), or your county office of education.

In the following section we'll look at the different types of agreements you'll need and illustrate some samples.

Enrollment Records and Policies

You will need certain kinds of information on each child you care for. A parent or guardian will supply the information, but you need a consistent form for recording and filing it. Each child's file should contain the following information:

- Child's full name, address, and phone number.
- Both parents' full names, home addresses, home phone numbers, workplace addresses, and phone numbers.
- Child's age and birth date.
- Child's doctor's name, phone number, and address.
- An adult emergency contact name and phone number (in the event that neither parent can be reached).
- A list of people who are authorized to pick the child up. Signatures must be obtained from these individuals, too.
- Any special provisions needed for the child.
- Date child began in care/date child left care.
- Medical consent form (see page 35).
- If you do not carry liability insurance, you need a written statement of disclosure to parents, with their signatures.
- Some states require you to give parents certain pamphlets and information on child abuse awareness; if so, you need signed receipts from them in the child's file.

Most providers find it wise to start every new child off on probationary terms. Not every child (or parent) will be happy and comfortable with your day care; nor will you be happy with every child. A trial period lets everyone know that a graceful "out" is available. Two weeks is a good trial time for child, parent, and provider. The agreement may be terminated any time during those two weeks. If all goes well, the agreement becomes a working arrangement and the child is accepted for regular enrollment.

Setting Your Fees

Your income is a crucial part of your business and one of the top reasons why you're opening a family child care. Take your time and do your research as you initially set your fees. Once you've set them, they can be changed, but it is much easier on provider and parents if you stick with these initial fees for a reasonable amount of time. We'll cover appropriate times to raise fees later in this chapter.

Weekly fees for children in family child care range widely. The fees generally depend on the number of hours children are in care, the area where you live, what other providers (both family child care and child care centers) are charging, the socioeconomic levels of the parents you are servicing, the age of the child, and the unique features of your family child care. Let's look closely at each of these.

- *The hours a child is in your care.* Obviously, if a child is with you part-time, the total fee will be proportionately less than for a full-time child. Do remember, however, that each child needs to bring in income for your business. If you're taking in two children for care after school, and you have no corresponding children to fill the morning, you've essentially filled spots for two full-time children at part-time fees. Many providers handle part-timers by charging a flat rate for full-time children and an hourly fee for part-time children. The hourly fee is usually greater than a full-time hourly fee would break down to be.
- *The area you live in.* Cities and urban areas generally have slightly higher fees than suburbs or rural areas. Fees are higher where the cost of living is higher. Call around to different child care facilities and find out what the fees are. Your local child care Resource and Referral agency can tell you what the average weekly fee for a full-time child is in your area.

- *What other child care in your area costs.* Your success depends somewhat on what the competition is charging. If Jane Q. Parent can get care for her child at $20 less a week at the local Children's Play-World, she may look less favorably on your establishment, no matter how enriching it is. You don't have to price yourself considerably lower than everyone else, but it is smart to be in the same general range to remain competitive.
- *Socioeconomic levels of parents.* If the parents in your community tend to hold blue-collar jobs, then you'll be charging less than if they hold management positions. It would be wonderful if we all had enough money to buy good child care at a price that truly reflects the service you provide, but the fact is, some of us do and some of us don't. The moral here is to know your market and get a feel for what families are capable of paying.
- *The age of the child.* Another fact of life: It's more time-consuming to care for an infant than it is to care for a preschooler. The state knows this too; they put limits on how many infants you may care for at any one time. Your fees should reflect the added work an infant brings you and the limits placed on your capacity. For newborns to two-year-olds an added fee is applicable.

    Debbie, a three-year veteran of family child care, describes her fees for infants.

    I charge $20 extra per week for a full-time infant. Right now I have a little boy, Joshua, age three, and his sister Rosalie, age seven months. The baby takes more constant care with diaper changes and such. I charge $80 per week for Joshua and $100 per week for Rosalie.
- *The unique features of your child care.* Every provider brings something special to her family child care. Your particular skills or the added effort you make may be worth an extra fee to parents. Anne, a provider with a small license, describes her fees.

    I'm a pediatric nurse who has chosen to stay home with my kids for a few years. Because of my medical background, I am uniquely qualified to care for children with special health problems or disabilities. My local R&R and the hospital I used to work at refer parents to me. Right now I have a little boy who is diabetic, a baby with cerebral palsy, and a little girl with a congenital heart condition. The diversity is wonderful for the children who can see that each and every one of us has special needs and is valuable. And the parents are much more comfortable knowing that I am trained to cope with medical needs and emergencies. My fees for these children are about 20 to 25 percent higher than what a more typical family child care would charge.

The special extra you provide doesn't have to be as sophisticated as Anne's special training. Perhaps you are willing to pick up children from school. Or maybe you hire a swimming instructor each summer to teach the children swimming and water safety. Your fees can reflect the added services you provide.

One last thing to remember is that parents are responsible for paying for the time they agree to use child care, *whether they bring their child or not.* A suggested policy on absences is covered below.

Some providers have a drop-in policy—meaning that if a regular child is absent, another child may take her place for the day for a flat fee. If the space is filled, the parent of the regular child is not charged for the day.

Late Fees

Despite their assurances and best intentions, parents will be late picking a child up from time to time. And some will be chronic offenders. Your best defense is a late fee policy. There are several ways to handle this. Eileen, an experienced provider, describes her policy this way.

My hours of operation are from 6:00 a.m. to 5:00 p.m. I don't encourage late pick-ups, but I do give parents fifteen minutes grace. If a parent arrives after 5:15 p.m., a late fee of $5 is charged for each fifteen-minute increment. If the parent knows he or she will be late and makes prior arrangements with me, a $3 fee per fifteen minutes is assessed.

Other providers give parents three late pick-ups for free, and then they start charging. You can decide what kind of system works best for you. One last note: Once you establish a late fee system, adhere to it strictly. If you do not follow through and charge late fees, parents will abuse your policy.

Payment Schedule

Payment schedules vary among family child care homes. It is best to require payment in advance. Some providers like to receive a check each Monday morning. Others will take payment every two weeks, and still others will take a check at the beginning of the month.

It is wise to include a sentence in your fee policy about bounced checks. This will happen occasionally, and if you have already covered bounced checks in the policies the parent reads and signs at the outset, you can deal with the problem in a calm, businesslike manner. Generally, providers allow for one or two bounced checks (assuming the check clears upon re-submission) as long as the parent covers the fee that is assessed to the provider's account. After this, the parent is required to pay the child care fees in cash and in advance.

Some providers accept cash only as payment. Payment policy is up to you.

Exceptions and Special Situations

Try not to include special situations and exceptions in your regular fee schedule; they can create problems with the other parents. But since life is unpredictable and some people may have legitimate (if unusual) needs, it is quite likely that you will make an exception for someone. Some providers will grant a special discount for two or more siblings in care at once. You might decide to bend your late fee schedule for emergency situations, or might even scale back your fee temporarily for someone who has lost a job.

An Addendum to the Parent-Provider Agreement:

Jones Family Child Care agrees to accept Tabitha Carr (age three), Jonathan Carr (age five), and Samantha Carr (age eighteen months) at the reduced rate of:

Jonathan: $60.00 per week (regularly $75.00)
Tabitha: $60.00 per week (regularly $75.00)
Samantha: $80.00 per week (regularly $90.00).

If, at any time, fewer than all three children attend, the rate will return to the full fee per week for each child present.

All other standard fee policies, late fees, vacation fees, meal fees, and any other special occasion fees apply, as stated in the parent-provider agreement.

This special rate agreement will be in effect until either party gives two weeks notice.

Provider:	Date:
Parent:	Date:

In any case, if you decide to make an exception, put it in writing with the parents involved and put limits on the allowance. For example, if you take on three children from one family and decide to give a "group discount," make sure you outline all the provisions to this policy. This agreement becomes an addendum to your basic parent-provider agreement (a full agreement is illustrated at the end of this chapter). The example above is how your special agreement might be worded.

Termination Policy

Since this is your business and livelihood, you need some notice if a child is to be withdrawn from care. The resulting loss of income needs to be planned for. Two weeks is a reasonable amount of notice to require if a parent plans to remove a child from child care. It is also standard to accept two weeks fee in lieu of notice.

Likewise, you also need to give notice if you plan to stop caring for a child. Except in cases of flagrant misconduct on the part of parent or child, give two weeks notice.

In cases of severe behavioral disturbance on the part of the child or parent, it is appropriate to terminate promptly. Care is commonly terminated when:

- A child hits, bites, or otherwise consistently hurts the other children.
- A child chronically "acts out" (e.g., swears, throws daily tantrums, or fails to comply with child care rules) to the point where the child may need therapeutic care.
- A child is genuinely unhappy and unable to adjust to being in child care.
- A parent routinely abuses drop-off and pick-up times.
- A parent doesn't pay the provider's bill on time or at all.
- A parent disagrees with the provider's guidance/discipline policy.
- A parent is unable or refuses to comply with ordinary requests for the child's well-being (for example, a request to send coat and boots with a child on a rainy day, to send diapers, to bathe the child, etc.).

Suspicion of child abuse is another legitimate reason child care is terminated. As a child care provider, you are mandated by most states to report any observed or suspected child abuse or neglect. If you are unsure about the seriousness of any incident or circumstance, you should phone your local Child Protective Services department. They can advise you on whether or not to make a report and investigate any report you do make. If you report a parent, you most likely will need to terminate care. A parent being reported in this way will be angry or defensive and too disruptive to continue servicing. If you have an unhappy and angry parent who removes a child from your care, it is wise to let your local child care Resource and Referral agency know about it. If they know the facts of the situation, it is less likely that any false accusations of abuse will be credited.

Hours of Operation

It is very important to state your hours of operation clearly. Your business is also your home and your family has a right to know when the children and parents will be there and when they can expect their home to be their own. Stating these hours up front, establishing and enforcing a late fee policy, and discouraging special situations will help keep your business from intruding on your family life.

Hours of operation vary widely among providers. You might have a fairly standard morning to early evening schedule, or you may have a nontraditional swing shift or graveyard schedule. In addition, some providers are open a regular five-day work week. Others are open four days a week, and still others are open on weekends.

Whichever portion of the working world you choose to service, it is important to remember that parents need time at the beginning of their "day" to get to work after dropping their children off, and at the other end of the day, they need time to get to your house after work. Some typical hours of operation are: 6:00 A.M.–5:30 P.M., 6:45 A.M.–5:15 P.M., 3:00 P.M.–11:30 P.M., or 7:00 A.M.–6:00 P.M. Any way you look at it, a successful family child care involves a long day.

Many providers find that putting a limit on the number of hours a child spends in care per day is helpful. It may be possible for you to care for a child for twelve hours a day, five days a week, but it is not good for you or the child. No more than ten hours a day (and less is preferable) in care is a good rule of thumb.

Holiday Schedule

It is standard practice in family child care to charge for national holidays that fall during your normal hours of operation. This means that you should be paid for at least the majority of the following holidays:

- Martin Luther King, Jr., Day
- Presidents Day
- Memorial Day
- Independence Day
- Labor Day
- Columbus Day
- Veteran's Day
- Thanksgiving (Thursday and Friday)
- Christmas Eve Day and Christmas Day
- New Year's Eve Day and New Year's Day.

Most providers charge for the above holidays when they fall on a regular work day. When one falls on a weekend, it is up to you whether you wish to charge for the holiday or not and take off the preceding Friday or following Monday.

Vacations

When a child goes on vacation, the parent needs to pay you something to "hold his spot." Generally, providers charge half the normal fee for child care for up to two weeks of vacation. It is wise to limit the amount of time you will hold a spot; economically, it's not smart for you to accept a half fee for more than two weeks when you could fill that spot with a full-fee child. In addition, require parents to give you at least one month's notice of any planned vacation of one week or more. You need to know if your income is going to vary.

When you go on vacation, there is generally no charge to the parent. Some providers even help arrange for alternate care. Plan your vacation well ahead of time and give all parents at least one month's notice. Many providers find it's helpful to go on vacation at the same time every year so the absence is more predictable for parents.

When the Children (or You) Get Sick

It's part of a child's job to build up his immunities by catching every little cold that comes along. But it's part of your job to ensure that a sick child doesn't share his illness. All the state usually says is that any child with a contagious disease must be separated from the rest of the children. Most providers take this policy a few steps further.

Laura, a provider with about two years experience, shares her policy.

> I ask parents to keep children home during the first two days of a bad cold or cough. I also ask parents to let me know if the child has been ill the day or night before coming to child care, even if she seems okay when she comes in; this way I can keep a good eye on her throughout the day. If a child is contagious, running a fever over 101°, throwing up, or has any other severe symptoms, I call the parents to take her home.

Remember that all the children deserve your attention. Sick children usually need extra attention and nurturing. If you cannot give such extra attention without short-changing the other children, then the sick child should be at home, not with you.

Some providers keep a list of babysitters who are willing to care for sick kids and provide these referrals to parents who can't stay home. It's a nice service when you aren't able to take in the sick children. Be sensitive to parents on this issue; almost all of them would prefer to stay home with their sick child, but many do not have such flexibility with their jobs. Be as accommodating as you can without endangering the other children.

If you are to administer medication to a child, the parent must bring it in its original bottle and make sure it is labeled with the child's name and the dosage instructions.

It's not just children who get sick, of course. Adults get sick too. And just as you don't want a sick child spreading chicken pox around, neither do you want to give everyone your own virus. It is smart to have a person lined up who can substitute for you in case of your illness. Deborah, a long-time provider with a large license, comments on this.

> I have my husband listed on my license so that I can have him substitute for me from time to time. This works well when I'm sick or if I need to be gone for a day to a training session or conference. He isn't a caregiver by profession, but he's a fun change for the children when he substitutes. My teenage assistant knows the daily schedule and will direct the activities for the day. My husband becomes the "responsible adult on the premises" and helps with whatever is needed.

Another option for finding a substitute is to check with your regional family child care support group. Many such groups are now compiling lists of available substitutes for providers.

In general, providers charge parents for the days their child is absent/sick and *do not* charge for the days the provider must close due to illness and has not provided a substitute.

Medical Consent Forms

Related to sick care is the form you need on hand in order to treat children for illness or emergency. It's basically a statement the parent signs, authorizing you to obtain medical care for her child if she is unreachable or if taking the time to find the parent would be a dangerous delay. Sample consent wording can be found on page 35 in chapter 2.

Meals

Most parents are interested in whether you plan to feed their children and many want to know what you will feed them. Some providers ask parents to bring the children's lunch, and then they serve the snacks. However, feeding six different children six different lunches can be quite time-intensive. And it can create food jealousy: "Hey! He's got Twinkies! I want some!"

Most providers supply all meals and snacks and include the expense in the weekly cost of care. Many books have been written on nutrition for young children and on meals for children in child care in particular. Later we will look at some sample menus and food ideas.

Remember that when you provide food for the children, you are eligible for reimbursement from CAFCP (see chapter 2). The food suppliers in your area will provide you with the program's requirements for nutritious food and documentation of what you serve and when.

Other Food Policies

When you supply all the meals and snacks for the children, it is advisable not to allow them to bring any candy, gum, chips, cookies, or other snacks to child care. What one child has, they all want. You can avoid such upheavals by making a "no non–child care supplied food" rule.

There are three general exceptions to this rule. First, providers usually require parents to bring formula and baby food for infants. Second, if a child requires a special diet for medical reasons, it is appropriate to ask the parent to supply it rather than have to prepare it yourself. Third, special occasions, like birthdays or Valentine's Day, are often enhanced by having parents bring in outside treats.

Guidance or Discipline

Let's face it: Most of the time, children do not behave like perfect little angels. It is your job to set limits and keep the children safe. Both child and parent need to know what to expect if a rule is broken. A written policy is helpful here, consisting of a brief statement outlining your guidance philosophy and preferred method of correcting children. For example: "At Sunshine Family Child Care we have rules to keep all children safe. If a child breaks a rule, we give short time-outs. If breaking rules becomes a persistent problem, we contact the parent and discuss other ways of handling the problem together."

Most providers like to use the time-out method of guidance. Time-out is a technique in which you remove a misbehaving child from the action and require her to sit quietly for a short time. The purpose is to remove the child from whatever stimulus is causing her to act out, give her the opportunity to calm down, and then to let her rejoin the group and try again. A more complete discussion of time-out, as well as other positive guidance methods, is offered in chapter 6.

Helen, a former preschool teacher and a provider with a small license, explains her philosophy:

> I care for two- and three-year-old children. The techniques I use with them are different because their level of understanding is different. With the three-year-olds, I use short periods of time-out (about three minutes) to remove them from the scene of conflict and help them regain control of their bodies and tempers. They know where the time-out spot is (a blue couch in the living room we call the "calm down couch"). When they come back, we talk briefly about what went wrong and what part of their behavior they need to change.
>
> The two-year-olds have a tendency to grab or hit automatically when thwarted and don't always pay attention to orders to stop. If this happens, I gently restrain them to keep them from hurting others or themselves. When they are calmer, I tell them what I want them TO DO. For example, I say, "Touch gently" rather than "Don't hit."

Other Policies You May Wish to Consider

Because each provider has a unique business and her own set of expectations, the policies and rules you set will differ from those of others. Here are some other issues for which you may wish to set a policy.

- *Potty training.* Some providers set rules for how old a child must be before they will assist with potty training (somewhere between twenty to thirty months is considered normal). In addition, it may also be necessary to ask parents to dress the child in easy-to-remove clothing (overalls and jumpsuits are frustrating for a child trying to make it to the bathroom in time). You may also want to require a supply of extra clothes and training pants. In general, the provider and parent must be in agreement as to how potty training will be approached. See page 72 for a sample policy on potty training.

    Note: A child is truly "potty-trained" when he is capable of using the toilet without an adult's presence or help and accidents are infrequent. Make sure you and the parents are clear about what stage the child is really in.

- *Clothing.* It's hard to believe, but many parents still dress their daughters for child care in fancy dresses and expect them to stay clean all day. Some parents also expect their sons not to get certain clothes dirty. It is sometimes necessary to explain to parents that young children learn by doing and "doing" is often a messy process. Art, cooking, science, and outdoor activities require clothing that is comfortable and washable. Children's learning is more important than their clothing; make sure parents support you on this one.

    Some providers like to require that a change of clothing be kept on hand for every child. Accidents happen from time to time; the child will be more comfortable if he's dry and reasonably clean.

- *Parking.* Some providers have special needs with regard to parking in their neighborhood. If you need parents to park in certain spots and avoid others, make it a policy. Your neighbors' good will is something to be preserved.

- *Pick-ups When Impaired.* Occasionally providers find it necessary to state in a policy that no child will be released to a parent who is obviously drunk, on drugs, or otherwise impaired in the provider's opinion. The child's safety is more important than the parent's "authority."

- *Child Care Philosophy.* Some providers find it helpful to include a statement of their child care philosophy along with their policies. It helps to give parents information about your background and approach and reassures them that their children are receiving quality care.
- *Communication.* It is helpful to state in your policies that you would like to know if there are special circumstances in a child's life (divorce, new sibling, other traumas) so that you can give that child the extra attention she needs. Likewise, it is helpful to invite parents to talk with you about any concerns they have about the care the child is receiving.

You've thought out all your policies and you've made notes to yourself. Now it's time to write them up and create your own Parent-Provider Agreement and Child Care Policies for parents to read and sign. Keep your policies simple and straightforward. Several examples of agreements and policies that other providers have found useful are illustrated on the following pages.

Strawberry Patch Child Care Policies

Child Care Philosophy

For the child:

1. To provide opportunities for being with other children in a setting conducive to the development of wholesome social relationships.
2. To provide appropriate play experiences that contribute to the developmental needs of the child.
3. To provide opportunities for meaningful play that is based on the child's individual needs, interests, handicaps, and abilities, and that will build important foundations for future skills.

For the parents:

1. To provide opportunities to meet with and work with other parents and teachers who have as their common concern the interests and needs of their children.
2. To provide care for the child while the parents pursue their own work or other interests.
3. To provide opportunities to grow in the understanding of child development.

For the community:

1. To help meet the needs of the community for an early childhood education facility.
2. To contribute to the wholesome growth and development of the citizens of the community.
3. To enhance the role of the Strawberry Patch Child Care as an integral part of the community.
4. To provide a setting where people of various religious and ethnic backgrounds can work together.

Schedule/Hours of Operation

1. The first ten days of care are probationary for provider, parent, and child. This agreement may be terminated any time during that period. Otherwise, two weeks notice is required if the child is to be permanently removed from this child care.

2. Two weeks fee will be accepted in lieu of two weeks notice, and, in fact, will be due with notice of plans to discontinue enrollment. Except in the case of gross misconduct on the part of either parent or child, provider will also tender two weeks notice prior to cessation of care. Your fee will be due when notice is given.

3. A charge of $5.00 per fifteen minutes, or any part thereof, will be charged for late pick-ups (anytime after 5:30) without prior consent of provider. You will be allowed three (3) overtimes (of not more than ten (10) minutes) per month before a late fee is charged. Once you have used up your three late pick-ups, you will be responsible for adding the late charge to your next paid fee. (Please do not ask if you owe an overtime charge when you know you have been later than five minutes or late more than three times in a month. It is embarrassing for both of us.) If arrangements have been made for late pick-up, the late fee will be based on a rate of $5.00 per half hour, or any part thereof, and will be due with your next paid fee.

4. *Children may be in attendance a maximum of ten (10) hours per day.*

5. Please understand: My 6:00 A.M.–5:30 P.M. schedule is only "child care hours" and does not reflect all of the additional hours necessary to provide quality day care. I am

here for you in case of emergency, but I do not want to work "overtime." If I am to do so, it must be worth my while. I too have a busy schedule that must be arranged around my providing child care services.

The following is my paid holiday schedule:
Martin Luther King, Jr., Day
Presidents Day
Memorial Day
Independence Day
Labor Day
Columbus Day
Veteran's Day
Thanksgiving Weekend (Thurs./Fri.)
Christmas Eve Day/Christmas Day
New Year's Eve Day/New Year's Day

6. There is no charge for any other time taken off by provider for vacation, sick days, or conferences. In case of emergency or illness, provider will make every attempt to provide substitute care. However, parents should be prepared with own backup.

Fees

1. Although family child care is a form of self-employ-ment, unlike other businesses, there is no room for growth or expansion due to licensing regulations. I do not receive any benefits that most employees take for granted, such as health insurance, paid sick days, vacation days or personal days, workman's compensation, retirement/pension plan, employment insurance, annual raises and bonuses. My contractual policies reflect this.
2. Fees are due in advance and payable no later than the first day of the week that your child attends. A $5.00 fee will be assessed if your fee is not paid on time and your child may not be accepted until your fee is paid, except under special circumstances prearranged and agreed to by provider.
3. Checks will be accepted. If, however, two checks are returned by the bank, your fee will be accepted in cash only. You will be responsible for any fees assessed to my account.

Vacation Guidelines

1. Parents are required to notify the Strawberry Patch two full weeks in advance when child is to be withdrawn to accompany parents on vacation. Parents then will be required to pay one half the regular week rate, in advance, for the vacation time in order to ensure readmission.
2. I will notify parents four weeks in advance of closure due to family vacation or an educational conference.

Meals

1. Breakfast, lunch, and two snacks are served each day at no additional charge.
2. Should your child arrive later than a meal time, you will be responsible for feeding him/her. Except for special

occasions or illness requiring a special diet, please do not send any food with your child. This includes, but is not limited to, gum, candy, chips, cookies, and cereal. Arrangements can be made for special days.

Sick Care

1. If your child is ill to the extent that it interrupts the care of or endangers the health of the other children, it will be necessary for you to make other arrangements for his/her care. Should your child become ill during his/her day here, you will be notified and we will determine the best course of action concerning appropriate care, which may include the child being taken home.
2. I will always respect your need to be at work when it comes to an ill child. I ask, however, that when deciding if your child should be at home, you give consideration to the other children in care and ask yourself how you would feel if your child were here and well and another child were as ill as your child is now.
3. My "bottom line" for not providing care is fever in excess of 101°, vomiting, excessive diarrhea, or any potentially contagious disorder. Further, there are times when a child is not that ill, but is terribly uncomfortable and really needs some "one on one" that I cannot provide and be fair to the other children. At those times I will strongly urge you to consider keeping your child at home.
4. Any medication to be given must come in a labeled prescription bottle. Nonprescription medicine, if needed, will also be administered, if provided by parent.

Guidance

1. Some people prefer to use the word "discipline" when discussing helping children learn to accept societal standards of behavior. However, the word "discipline" frequently has a connotation of punishment, which makes it

less desirable in our educational setting. That is, the question, "how do you discipline your child?" usually translates into, "how do you punish your child?" In the education setting and with a developmental philosophy of early childhood education, the word "guidance" is more accurate.

2. When appropriate, children will be given short periods of "time out" for guidance.

Potty Training

1. Potty Trained: The child is capable of using the toilet, but it is the adult who is trained to get the child to the bathroom on time. Accidents occur often. It is the first step in the total process.

2. Potty Learned: The child is not only capable of using the toilet, but has the developmental ability to express the need to go. Accidents occur, but infrequently.

3. If potty training is begun when your child is ready, the task is easy and quick. If parents undertake the task of potty training when *they* want it to happen, the task is arduous and painful for all concerned. Thirty months of age is a good rule of thumb to start checking for signs of readiness.

4. When we agree that the time is right for your child and until he/she is totally successful in his/her toileting, NO wearing of overalls or clothing with suspenders, snaps, buckles, belts or zippers. Elastic waisted pants ONLY. Anything else sets your child up for failure. In addition, your child's locker box MUST have two complete changes of clothes and several pairs of thick training pants. If your child does not have immediate success, he/she will be put back into diapers and after a respite, the process will be attempted again. This does not harm the child in any way; in fact, keeping a child in "grown-up" pants when he or she is not successful is harmful.

Activities

1. Creativity is the basis for all activities at the Strawberry Patch.
2. Creativity integrates physical, mental, social, and emotional growth. Creativity is fostered by a free, flexible, accepting, and open environment and by openly discovering, inventing, and creating. In addition to having the opportunity for self-expression, children are practicing small motor skills, eye-hand coordination, left to right progression, and whole-part relationships.

Miscellaneous

1. Any changes in personal address or phone numbers will be given to provider as soon as possible. Names and phone numbers on emergency forms will be kept current.
2. Note that your child will only be released to persons other than the parent or legal guardian if their name appears on your signed emergency form. In case of an emergency a phone call from you will suffice as long as the person picking up the child shows identification.
3. All possible care is taken to provide a safe and healthy environment; however, children do have accidents. I am certified in Pediatric CPR and have Red Cross training. In case of an accident I will: tend to the child, notify the parent. In case of an emergency I will: tend to child, call 911, notify parent. Your child will be taken to Grossmont Hospital if that becomes necessary. It is incumbent upon you to check with the Hospital Emergency Room to find out what kind of forms they require to be on file for treatment in case of parental absence.
4. I am a mandated reporter of suspected child abuse. Your child's welfare will ALWAYS come first. I will con-

sult with you if possible. Please understand that I have few options.

5. Any person picking up your child in an impaired condition (in my estimation inebriated or on drugs) will be encouraged to allow me to find alternate transportation. I cannot legally withhold a child from a legal guardian but if I feel a child is in jeopardy I will not hesitate to contact the police.

6. Open communication is the key to a happy, long-lasting relationship between a child care provider and her child care families. Please do not ever hesitate to contact me about anything that affects the well-being of your child.

Day-Care Policies and Procedures
Camille's Day Care

Admission Requirements and Enrollment Procedures

A. Each child must visit my home for one-half hour before placement to help reduce separation fears and to see how the child will fit in.

B. If we agree that the child will be placed, the parents must provide the following:
   1. A completed registration form.
   2. A complete record of age-required immunizations.
   3. Authorization to receive emergency medical care.
   4. Date of last physical exam.
   5. Authorization to transport the child in my van.
   6. Authorization for field trips, walks, etc.

Hours of Operation

A. The day care will operate Monday through Thursday from 7:30 A.M. to 5:30 P.M.

B. *Day-Care Holiday Schedule*

Labor Day	Sept. 7 (Monday)
Thanksgiving	Nov. 26 (Thursday)
Winter break	Dec. 21–Jan. 1
Martin Luther King, Jr. Day	Jan. 18 (Monday)
Presidents Day	Feb. 15 (Monday)
Spring break	April 12–13 (Monday & Tuesday)
Memorial Day	May 31 (Monday)
Summer break	To be announced

I have read and agree to these policies and procedures.

(Please initial) _____ Date _____

C. You will be charged for all days you agree to have your child attend day care. If your child does not attend you will be charged the minimum daily rate (see below). There is no charge for days when the day care is closed.

D. I will give one month notice if I feel the day care arrangement needs to be terminated.

E. I would appreciate notice if you plan to discontinue day care, but it is not required.

F. In case of emergency, illness, or other situations that would result in my absence, I have two qualified women who can fill in for me.

Payment Plans and Fees

A. *Fee Schedule Effective September 1–August 31:*

Children 12–18 months	$3.00 per hour
Children 18–24 months	$2.80 per hour
Children 2 years and over	$2.60 per hour
Second child	$2.30 per hour
Third child	$2.00 per hour
Minimum per day for one child	$18.50
Minimum per day for two children	$35.50

B. There is a late fee after 5:30 P.M. of $3.00 per fifteen minutes.

C. Charges are based on the time you have arranged to leave your child to the time you actually pick up on the half hour. For example, if you have arranged to drop off your child at 8:30 A.M., you will then be charged from that time even if you drop off later. You will then be charged on the half hour when you pick up; e.g., if you pick up at 4:15 P.M., you will be charged for 4:30 P.M.

I have read and agree to these policies and procedures.

(Please initial) _____ Date _____

D. You will be charged for the time your child is in another program (preschool, dancing lessons, etc.) since a place is kept open for him or her during that time.

E. This fee covers all meals, diapers, preschool supplies, and field trips.

F. You will be billed on the fifteenth and last day of the month. Your payment is due within a week unless other arrangements have been agreed upon.

G. Rates will be evaluated in June. You will be notified of any changes in July, and any rate changes will be effective on September 1.

Typical Daily Schedule

A. Meal Times:
>   Breakfast—7:30 to 8:30 A.M.
>   Morning snack—9:30 to 10:00 A.M.
>   Lunch—11:30 to noon
>   Afternoon snack—3:30 to 4:00 P.M.

B. Napping and/or quiet time—1:00 to 3:00 P.M. (Children under eighteen months will be on a demand schedule.)

C. Daily schedule will include:

1. Free-play activities (large variety of toys).

2. Outdoor play (riding toys, swings, climbing toys, slides, teeter-totter, merry-go-round, large sandbox, and grassy area for running and ball play).

3. Small muscle play (Duplos; blocks; waffle blocks; puzzles; beads to string; pegboards; stacking, sorting, and nesting toys; super maze; construction sets; Lincoln Logs; Brio train; mini and micro cars; small dolls, etc.).

4. Preschool activities include painting, coloring, cutting, gluing, play dough, etc. A theme is followed every

---

I have read and agree to these policies and procedures.

(Please initial) _____ Date _____

month starting with the colors in the fall. The shapes, some numbers, and letters are covered, interspersed with the different seasons and holidays arts and crafts.
5. Stories, songs, rhymes, and music.
6. Creative play (dress-up clothes, dolls, dishes, puppets, etc.).
7. Television watching will be kept to a minimum and will vary depending on the weather, mood of the children, etc. Only PBS, Disney, children's videos, and some cartoons will be watched.

Meals and Snacks

A. All meals, snacks, and drinks will be provided.
B. All beverages will be 100% fruit juice or 2% milk. Bread products will be whole wheat or partially whole wheat. Cheese will be unprocessed. No sugar cereals and sweet drinks will be served. Other sweets and treats will be kept to a minimum.
C. Meals and snacks will be nutritional and the daily menu will follow the guidelines recommended by the USDA child care food program.
D. A weekly menu will be posted.
E. Birthday and holiday treats will be provided by the day care. Children are not permitted to bring gum, candy, or other treats.

Discipline Policy

A. A "time out" chair will be used for aggressive, disruptive, or destructive behavior for children over two years old. Children under two will be distracted and guided to other activities.

I have read and agree to these policies and procedures.

(Please initial) _____ Date _____

B. My house is very childproofed and there are very few things that are off-limits to the children. I feel that exploring and "getting into things" are a normal and healthy part of childhood.

C. A well organized, well supervised, and stimulating atmosphere will be provided that should minimize any need for discipline. If a discipline problem should arise involving your child, we will discuss the problem and work out a solution together.

D. Corporal punishment of any type will not be used.

Transportation

A. Your child will be transported only in an automobile in safe operating condition that is covered by insurance and operated by a licensed and safe driver.

B. Your child will at times be in a seat belt or other protective device suitable for his/her age and weight.

C. There will be occasional field trips to the local parks or zoo. There will be at least one adult for every four children. No additional fees or equipment (other than regular outdoor wear) will be required for field trips. You will be notified of any field trips in advance, and I will try to let you know if I will be transporting your child for any other reason.

Health Policies and Procedures

A. Medical Emergencies
   1. Immediate first aid will be given.
   2. An ambulance will be called and the recommendations of the paramedics followed.

I have read and agree to these policies and procedures.

(Please initial) _____ Date _____

3. Parents will be notified as soon as possible. If you are not available, other family or friends on your registration form will be notified.

4. Parents are responsible for any expenses incurred as a result of emergency room care, ambulance, etc.

5. Hospitals used for emergencies:

NORTHWEST HOSPITAL   STEVENS HOSPITAL
1550 N. 155th   21600-76th Ave. W.
364–0500   774–0555

B. First Aid Procedures

1. First aid will be in accordance with the Red Cross first aid class and the Poison Center.

2. Everyone who cares for your child takes an EMERGENCY CARE AND CPR FOR INFANTS AND CHILDREN course each year.

3. A complete first aid kit, syrup of ipecac, ice packs, and emergency numbers will be kept on the premises.

4. Parents will be notified of all accidents and a record of injuries will be kept on each child.

C. Illness

1. If your child becomes ill during the day, you will be notified and are expected to pick up your child as soon as possible.

2. If your child will be missing day care due to illness, please notify me by phone in the morning or the previous evening.

D. Communicable Disease Prevention and Reporting

1. Your child will be kept isolated from other children as much as possible if your child has a communicable disease. Communicable diseases will be reported to the Department of Health.

2. Each child will be observed daily for illness.

I have read and agree to these policies and procedures.

(Please initial) _____ Date _____

3. Individual bedding, towels, washcloths, glasses, etc., will be used to minimize spreading infections.

E. Handwashing, Diapering, Sanitizing & Laundering Policies

1. Day care provider will wash hands before and after diapering; toileting; eating, handling, and preparing food; and handling contaminated materials.

2. Children will wash after toileting, after handling contaminated materials, and before and after eating.

3. Diapers will be changed regularly and immediately after a bowel movement. Bottoms will be thoroughly cleaned and corn starch or petroleum jelly will be used as needed. Other types of preparations must be provided by parents.

4. The diapering area will be sanitized after each use; contaminated utensils and toys will be sanitized.

5. Bedding will be laundered as needed or once a week.

6. Bottles and nipples will be washed in the dishwasher and rinsed again with hot water before filling.

F. Medication Management

1. All prescribed medication must be labeled with the child's name and must be accompanied by written permission from the parent to dispense.

2. As-needed medications must be labeled with the child's name and must be accompanied by written permission from the parent to dispense.

G. Health Records

1. Immunization records and the date of your child's last physical examination must be kept up-to-date.

2. Please notify me of any special health problems or concerns regarding your child or family.

I have read and agree to these policies and procedures.

(Please initial) _____ Date _____

Religious Activities

A. A simple blessing will be said before meals to help settle children.
B. Religious music (e.g., Christmas carols) may be played or sung.

Non-Discrimination Policy

No child will be discriminated against on the basis of race or religion.

Miscellaneous Information

A. Parents have free access to all areas of my house and yard that are used by their children.
B. Children are discouraged from bringing their own toys, and the day care is not responsible for any that are broken or lost. Security blankets and/or toys and pacifiers are welcome.
C. No smoking is allowed in the day care house or yard at any time.
D. Parents are free to call at any time to see how their child is doing. An answering machine will be used at times to avoid interruptions, but I will return your call as soon as possible.
E. Fire drills will be conducted monthly and recorded on the evacuation plan that is posted on the entry bulletin board.
F. As a day care provider I am required to report any suspected child abuse or neglect.
G. The schools that serve this area are St. Luke, Crista, Syre, and Sunset. None of these schools are within

---

I have read and agree to these policies and procedures.

(Please initial) _____ Date _____

walking distance for young children. However, there are city and school buses that serve these schools.

H. Parents are encouraged to discuss their child with me at any time, or to call in the evening or on weekends. Good communication is essential to good day care and happy children.

_____

I/We have read and agree to these policies and procedures for the care of my/our child/children.

Parent _____

Date _____

Parent _____

Date _____

Provider _____

Date _____

4

Your Daily Schedule

In planning a daily schedule for your child care, you will need to consider three variables: the age-mix of the children, your background and training, and your temperament.

Age-mix of the Children

Ages of children can be generally defined as follows: Birth to one year = infant; one to two years = toddler; three to five years = preschooler. If you specialize in infants, your daily schedule will differ from that of providers who care for toddlers and preschoolers. Infants take an enormous amount of caregiving time, typically do not interact much with each other, and have limited attention spans. Toddlers are endlessly active, take a great deal of monitoring, have short attention spans, and play more alongside of other children than with them. Toddlers need a lot of intervention from you since they are not yet capable of sharing. Preschoolers have a good grasp of language, an attention span long enough for most activities, adore playing with each other, and need direction more than intervention.

Since most providers have a mix of ages, this chapter will look at the components of a schedule geared for children ages eighteen months to four years.

Your Background and Training

Perhaps you have just spent two years working as a preschool teacher, or have had schooling in early childhood education. If so, then you have a wonderful background with which to begin a toddler and/or preschool curriculum of activities, including art, science, learning games, and more.

Or maybe you're a parent with a well-established routine for feeding and keeping the children occupied—you know it works and you plan to adapt it to child care. Whatever your background, it will influence your choices for how to structure the day.

Your Temperament

All of us have different personalities. Some providers have a strong need for structure. Other providers like to be spontaneous and change activities quickly if the situation seems to warrant it. Children do best with a mixture of both qualities from adults. They need to know what to expect in care and they also need a provider flexible enough to switch gears if an activity is not stimulating or if it gets out of hand. Most providers strike a balance between structure and spontaneity early on.

Devising a Daily Schedule

Your daily schedule will always include mealtimes, naptime, free play, and structured play. Welcoming time and storytime are also commonly included in the day. Here are a few sample daily schedules from experienced providers:

Nichols Family Child Care

(Capacity: 6 kids, ages 4–5)

Hours of Operation	8:00 A.M.–5:00 P.M.
Breakfast	8:00–9:00 A.M.
Circle time and welcoming activities	9:00–9:30 A.M.
Preschool project	9:30–10:00 A.M.
Snack time	10:00–10:20 A.M.
Free play	10:20–11:05 A.M.
Outdoor games	11:05 A.M.–noon
Handwashing	noon–12:15 P.M.
Lunch	12:15–1:00 P.M.
Naptime/Quiet time	1:00–1:30 P.M.
Story time	1:30–1:50 P.M.
Structured play	1:50–2:35 P.M.
Afternoon snack	2:35–3:00 P.M.
Free play/outdoor play	3:00–4:00 P.M.
Closing circle time	4:00–4:30 P.M.
Clean-up	4:30–5:00 P.M.

Moore Family Child Care

(Capacity: 12 kids, ages 18 months–6 years)

Hours of Operation	6:00 A.M.–5:30 P.M.
Arrival/Free play	6:00–8:00 A.M.
Breakfast	8:00–8:30 A.M.
Circle time	8:30–9:00 A.M.
Music/Math	9:00–9:25 A.M.
Outdoor play	9:25–10:00 A.M.
Morning snack	10:00–10:15 A.M.
Creative art	10:15–10:45 A.M.
Free play	10:45–11:30 A.M.
Language games	11:30 A.M.–noon
Lunch	noon–12:30 P.M.
Rest time	12:30–2:30 P.M.
Wake-up/Video	2:30–3:15 P.M.
Afternoon snack	3:15–3:30 P.M.
Outdoor play/Homework	3:30–4:30 P.M.
Free play/Pick-up	4:30–5:30 P.M.

Bakeman Family Child Care	
(Capacity: 12 kids, ages 3–5 years)	
Hours of Operation	7:30 A.M.–5:30 P.M.
Breakfast	7:30–8:30 A.M.
Free play	8:30–9:30 A.M.
Morning snack	9:30–10:00 A.M.
Small-muscle play	10:00–10:30 A.M.
Preschool activities	10:30–11:00 A.M.
Music time	11:00–11:30 A.M.
Lunch	11:30 A.M.–noon
Free play	noon–12:30 P.M.
Story time	12:30–1:00 P.M.
Naptime/Quiet time	1:00–3:00 P.M.
Outdoor play	2:00–3:30 P.M.
Afternoon snack	3:30–4:00 P.M.
Creative play	4:00–4:30 P.M.
Free play	4:30–5:00 P.M.
Video watching	5:00–5:30 P.M.

Mealtimes: An Essential Part of the Day

You'll notice in each of the above schedules, providers carefully space food breaks about two to three hours apart. If you let children get hungry, they get cranky and act out. Regular, predictable meal times are essential.

What to Feed the Kids

Your local food program supplier will give you a plethora of material on suggested foods and menus. Many publish their own cookbooks, which are filled with nutritious, fun, day-care–tested recipes. In addition, there are many books available on child care (including family child care) that have excellent sections on nutrition and suggested recipes. You'll find a list of these resources in the Appendix.

Tina, a provider for about one year, has this to say about preparing meals.

> My partner and I plan a weekly menu ahead of time. Then we post it for parents to see. We have two children with dietary restrictions, so those parents scrutinize it carefully. Spencer, age four, has PKU and can't have protein. His parents supply his protein substitutes and formula and we supplement with vegetables and fruit. Amanda, age three, has a milk allergy, so we have to monitor her as well.
>
> I used to pretty much prepare the same kinds of meals each week. Then we bought a cookbook from our food supplier. I spent an hour one day going through it and picking out dishes I could make easily and the kids would like. This has been very successful. The kids like the variety and the fun day-care touches (e.g., peanut butter sandwiches cut out with a heart cookie cutter). And because the cookbook is supplied by the food program, I know the recipes are nutritionally sound.

The food programs can give you up-to-date information on how much kids should eat and from which food groups. It is sometimes surprising to learn how little the portions for young children really are. Familiarize yourself with the recommended amounts of food for children of different ages.

You don't need to prepare elaborate meals for young children. The simpler the meals are to prepare, the better. Children will benefit more from your guidance and presence in their play than they will from having you cook for long periods in the kitchen.

Camille, a provider of five years, talks about simplicity in the kitchen.

> I only get a couple kids for breakfast, so I keep it very simple—just oatmeal or another cereal, and fruit and milk. I shop every two weeks and I repeat menus frequently to keep the workload down. My husband drives home by a bakery outlet, so he stops for me once a week to pick up whole-grain bread. It took me a little while to familiarize myself with the food

program's guidelines (e.g., no processed cheese, Campbells soup, Spaghetti-Os, frozen pizza, etc.) and with the children's tastes (they like milder tasting things, like albacore tuna), but once I got it all down, I shopped much more quickly. Because the food program covers pretty much all my food expenses, I don't economize heavily.

The following is a short list of tried and true, favorite snacks and dishes compiled by family child care providers. It is by no means complete, but it can give you a bit of a head start when it comes to planning meals or jog you out of the afternoon snack rut of crackers and juice. Sample menus are also included.

Breakfast	*Lunch*	*Snacks*
Cold cereal	Sloppy Joes	Quesadillas (flour
Hot cereal with	Cheese slices	tortillas)
strawberries	Scrambled eggs	Soft pretzels
Peanut butter toast	Homemade pizza	Tortilla chips & salsa
Oatmeal	Macaroni and cheese	Granola bars
Fresh fruit kebobs	Tuna sandwiches	Fruit cocktail
Yogurt	Black beans and rice	Dried fruit
Bran muffins	Rice pudding	Carrot sticks
Hard-boiled eggs	Grilled cheese	Celery stuffed with
with relish	sandwiches	peanut butter
Waffles/pancakes	Vegetable soup	Banana bread
		Applesauce

The following are sample menus providers use and make available to parents. You'll notice the sample menu also functions as a recordkeeping document for the CACFP (each food supplier has a variation on this form and can supply you with it). The menu also provides information on recommended daily portions of the food groups for young children (also courtesy of the food supplier).

Sample Menu

Breakfast	Lunch	Snacks
Pancakes Orange juice	Spaghetti (from scratch) Peaches Green beans Milk	Muffin/butter Milk
Eggs Toast Apple juice Milk	Tuna sandwich Carrot sticks Orange slices Milk	Crackers/ spread Milk or juice
French toast Pears Milk	Cheese and ham sandwich Celery sticks Apple slices Milk or juice	Banana bread Cream cheese Milk
Waffles Applesauce Milk	Macaroni and cheese Hot dogs (all meat) Fruit salad Milk	Grapes Crackers and cheese Milk or juice
Cereal Banana Muffin Milk	Bean burritos Lettuce and tomato Oranges Milk	Carrot bread Milk or juice
Hot oatmeal Cantaloupe Toast Milk	Omelette Roll/butter Pears Carrots Milk	Raisins Crackers and cheese Milk or juice
English muffins Melted cheese Juice Milk	Toasted cheese sandwich Apples Broccoli Milk	English muffins Peanut butter Milk or juice

Date:			Monday
Record Daily Attendance: *			ATT _____
Amount Age 1-2	Amount Age 3-6		Food Items
¼ cup	½ cup	**Breakfast** Vegetable or fruit or juice	*Corn Chex fruit cocktail milk*
½ slice	½ slice	Bread / Equivalent or	
¼ cup	⅓ cup	Cereal	
½ cup	¾ cup	Milk	#
See Snack Sheets for Amounts		**AM Snack** Choose 1 Item from 2 Groups: Meat, Bread, Milk, Fruit-Veg	*soft pretzels milk* #
1 oz.	1½ oz.	**Lunch** Meat and/or Meat Alternate	*tuna sandwich (tuna, whole wheat bread) broccoli, fruit cocktail , milk*
¼ cup Total	½ cup Total	2 Fruits or 2 Vegetables or 1 of each	
½ slice	½ slice	Bread/Equivalent	
½ cup	¾ cup	Milk	#
See Snack Sheets for Amounts		**PM Snack** Choose 1 Item from 2 Groups: Meat, Bread, Milk, Fruit-Veg	*cottage cheese fruit cocktail milk* #
1 oz.	1½ oz.	**Dinner** Meat and/or Meat Alternate	
¼ cup Total	½ cup Total	2 Fruits or 2 Vegetables or 1 of each	
½ slice	½ slice	Bread/Equivalent	
½ cup	¾ cup	Milk	#
See Snack Sheets for Amounts		**Eve Snack** Choose 1 Item from 2 Groups: Meat, Bread, Milk, Fruit-Veg	#

Note: Where you see the symbol # please enter the number of children claimed at this meal. See the RVDCH Handbook for amounts for ages 6–12.

Tuesday ATT _____	Wednesday ATT _____	Thursday ATT _____	Friday ATT_____
Food Items	Food Items	Food Items	Food Items
Cream of Wheat strawberries milk #	Rice Chex pears milk #	whole wheat toast w/ peanut butter and honey, milk #	Rice Krispies mandarin oranges milk #
Rice Krispies milk #	rice cakes milk #	wheat hearts milk #	peanut butter toast milk #
Sloppy Joes (Sloppy Joe mix, hamburger, hamburger buns, tomato paste), carrots, pears, milk #	peanut butter and jelly sandwiches, green beans, pineapple, slice of cheese, milk #	vegetable soup cheese slices Saltine crackers mandarin oranges, milk #	scrambled eggs whole wheat toast cheese pears, corn milk #
Granola bars milk #	whole wheat toast milk #	graham crackers raisins #	Cheerios milk #
#	#	#	#
#	#	#	#

Making Mealtime a Pleasant Experience

Family child care means care in a family setting. This applies to mealtime, too. Meals and snacks will be more enjoyable for all concerned if both you and the children sit around a table and make it a group or "family" experience. One provider takes it a step further.

> I put it in my policy that we will say a short, non-denominational blessing over each meal or snack. I think it helps the kids settle down, appreciate the food, and eat it in a more family-like atmosphere. It also helps emphasize manners.

Another provider creates a family atmosphere by having the children help serve the food. Others prefer to set food on the table in serving dishes and allow children to serve themselves, as feasible.

Tips for Mealtime

Many children are fussy eaters. In general, providers agree that it's best not to cater to a picky eater. Don't go looking for a substitute food if a child says he hates peanut butter and won't eat his sandwich. Don't worry; he'll eat at the next meal or snack, and after a while, will learn to like different foods.

Children accept new foods more easily if they look appetizing and are presented in small portions. Again, be patient with children's tastes.

Never force a child to eat something or punish him for not cleaning his plate. Try not to withhold a treat or dessert for any reason. Some educators believe using food this way gives it an exaggerated importance.

When it comes to clean-up, one provider has this tip:

> In the interests of reducing work and preventing accidents, I use tippy cups (a child-size plastic cup with a snap-on lid and a drinking spout—you can get them from Tupperware) for all the children, no matter what age. The cup is labeled with the child's name and she uses it all day long.

Mealtime becomes even more fun when children are allowed to help prepare some of the dishes. In chapter 5 we'll look at cooking with children.

Naptime

As a general guideline, all children up to age five should take a nap (or "rest") during the day. Obviously, infants nap more frequently and for more of the day. Children vary widely in how well they go down for a nap, how well they sleep (if at all), and how long they sleep.

You will do well to manage these differences by insisting that everyone nap or rest at the same time, every day. There are some children who just won't go to sleep or who wake early. Most providers handle this by telling them they can "just rest their bones" but they must stay on their mats or beds and not talk or play. Other providers care for older children who have given up rest time for good; these children are commonly allowed to stay up and do "quiet-time" activities, like reading, while the other children sleep.

Sleep habits in child care are generally influenced strongly by the child's sleep habits at home. If a child is accustomed to waking frequently and crying for Mom, having three glasses of water before bed, or having a parent lie down with her, then there will be a period of adjustment—and probably resistance—before the child settles down to your routine.

Having a routine and sticking to it will make naptime refreshing for everyone. Parents will also appreciate picking up a child who is not cranky and overtired at the end of the day.

Free Play

You'll enjoy devising your own mixture of free, or independent, play opportunities. Be sure to include indoor as well as outdoor play and all the toys that go with them.

Playing Outside and Inside

Brenda, a provider for five years with a large license, talks about what her kids like best:

> For some reason I've always had a lot of boys in care. So I schedule as much free outdoor play as possible. When they are playing outdoors, the children's favorite things to play with are the swings and sandbox. I encourage sandbox play and give them water, scooping utensils, and buckets. They do tend to track in sand, but the learning they get out of it is worth it. I found they lost interest quickly in the expensive ride-on toys I bought. If I had to do it over again, I would have built a bigger sandbox and skipped the Big Wheels.

Outdoor play is doubly useful in that the exercise tires the children out before nap/quiet time, they sleep better, and they tend to get along with others better.

Indoor play is no less enjoyable for children. Jan, a new provider with a small license, lives in a state where the weather is often rainy.

> Because of the weather, we have to stay inside much of the year. My kids' favorite free-play areas are the construction toy area (I have a big Duplo train they can take apart and put back together) and the doll corner. They also love the book nook, where they can curl up with a favorite book on big pillows.

Tina, a provider of one year, tells about how she facilitates smooth play during free-play time.

> I make it a rule that no more than three or four kids can play in any one play area at a time. It cuts down on sharing problems and space issues. The kids really do respect the rule.

Toys

As young children learn through play, toys are natural learning tools. Providers are wise to select toys carefully for high-interest and long-term use.

Children do tire of the same toys after a while. One way to

deal with this is to rotate the toys available. Bring out the construction toys for a few days, then put those away and bring out the dress-up clothes, followed by a doll house, and so on. Watch to see when the children's interest flags and then make the change for the next day. You'll get a feel for how long each toy entertains.

Camille, an experienced provider, offers these tips:

> First, don't use toy boxes. When the toys are all in a jumble, kids are not attracted to them. If they are organized neatly on low shelves, children are much more likely to play with them.
>
> Second, change your main room around every so often. For whatever reason, finding the block area in a different corner of the room makes block play fresh and alluring. An added bonus is that it evens out the wear and tear on your carpet.

Parents often complain that their young children vastly prefer to play with pots and pans in the kitchen, or with big empty boxes, rather than with the beautiful new toys eagerly purchased for them. You can avoid this problem to a certain extent by tuning into children's interests, being aware of their developmental capabilities, and educating yourself on the purpose of play before you buy the toys.

Here are a few criteria to keep in mind as you go about selecting toys for children:

- Make sure the toy is safe for the age you intend it for. Infants shouldn't play with toys that have small pieces or parts that can be swallowed, or with toys that have long strings that could get wrapped around their necks. Toys with sharp edges, that have lead paint on them, or that contain hidden wires are all hazardous to young children. Most toys have a recommended age range printed on the package.
- A toy needs to be challenging to the child without frustrating him. For instance, a toddler isn't developmentally ready for a puzzle of more than two or three pieces.
- Try to have a good selection of open-ended toys for children, that is, toys that can be used for more than one type of play. For example, paint, blocks, or dolls can be played with in many ways. A coloring book, though, has one use and one

use only. When the toy is open-ended, you give children permission to stretch their imaginations in play.

- Toys should match the children's current interests. Many preschoolers are passionately interested in dinosaurs. One provider purchased a set of small, sturdy plastic dinosaurs and then gave the children a box of items to create an environment for the dinosaurs. The children made roads and houses out of Lincoln Logs, trees and caves from Play Dough, and then brought out some small Flintstones characters to play with the dinosaurs. The plastic dinosaurs matched their current interest and obviously the children were quite capable of extending the play.
- The toys you choose need to be well-made and hold long-term interest for the children. Open-ended toys, for example, blocks, tend to be best for this.
- Be sensitive to sex-role stereotyping and racial bias in toys. Not every traditional "girl-toy" needs to be pink, pretty, and passive. And not every traditional "boy-toy" needs to be army green and destructive. You want the children to play with the opposite sex as well as with same-sex friends and you want them to engage both in nurturing play and action play. A good selection of nonstereotyped toys will encourage this. In addition, scrutinize your doll collection and play figures carefully; are they all blond and Caucasian? Children need to see a variety of ethnic backgrounds, even if you service only one type of family.

Toys for Babies

Many toys for babies are created to appeal more to the parents who buy them than to the children who play with them. Babies are far likelier to prefer common household items, which make terrific toys.

Here is a list of items you probably already have on hand, all of which are perfect for babies to play with:

Tennis balls
Shoeboxes

Nesting measuring spoons and cups
Cardboard tubes (paper towel or toilet paper)
Pie tins
Colored sponges
Wooden and plastic spoons
Old purse
Pots and pans with covers
Bells (big enough not to be swallowed)
Drawers or cupboard doors to open and close

And here are some simple toys you can purchase:

Blocks (wooden or soft)
Stuffed animals
Color cone (graduated rings on a post)
Music box
Plastic shapes (circle, square, triangle) that can be dropped into
    a box with same shape holes
Pail and shovel
Dolls
Jack-in-the-box

Toys for Toddlers

Toddlers are very busy, have short attention spans, and touch everything. They are attracted to many things, but don't stay with them for very long.

As with babies, toys don't need to be elaborate or expensive; many popular toddler toys are simple, household items. Toddlers like fairly realistic toys—a vehicle that looks like a bus, or a doll that looks like a baby.

Here are some playthings you may already have on hand:

Sand
Water and cups for filling and dumping
Rocks (medium-sized) to put into containers and dump out
Empty bandage boxes
Old telephone
Safe kitchen utensils and bowls

Dress-up clothes
Plastic dishes
A big cardboard box
Soap bubbles and wands

And here are some toddler-tested toys you may wish to pur-chase:

Blocks
Dolls
Puzzles with big pieces
Stuffed animals
Stacking toys
Cars/trains/trucks/buses/airplanes
Duplos (toddler-sized construction blocks)
Rubber or soft balls
Housekeeping toys (stove, sink, etc.)
Screw toys

Toys for Preschoolers

Now some serious imagination begins to show itself. Whereas a toddler will play with an airplane by making it fly with some ac-companying engine sounds, a preschooler will turn a jumbo crayon into a jet and explain that it has no propeller. Dramatiza-tion is also coming on strong and many preschoolers use toys as props in their dramatic play.

Preschoolers' fine motor skills have increased so that they are much more capable of manipulating smaller objects and con-struction toys. But they still love playing with big toys. Their play becomes much more cooperative; they are now interested in other children's ideas and suggestions for play rather than pro-tecting a toy from them. They become more interested in how different toys can fit or work together, thus construction toys and Lincoln Logs are now popular.

Karen shares how she observed this combining behavior in two of her four-year-olds.

Tyler and Alexa were playing with miniature cars. First they built a track for the cars out of flat blocks and then they hitched up a little toy wagon from another set of toys to one car. "It's a trailer!" they told me.

You'll notice that many preschoolers spend more time talking about playing, deciding what to play, and directing who does what than actually playing.

Here are a few items preschoolers like to play with that you might have around the house:

Large appliance boxes (be sure to remove all staples)
Flashlights
Soap bubbles and wands
Baskets
Boards for balancing on
Unopened, discarded junk mail
Dress-up clothes (including pieces of fabric for capes and veils)
Costume jewelry
Sandbox
Suitcases
Empty food containers—oatmeal boxes, milk cartons, etc.
Blankets, pillows

Here are some toys for preschoolers you might like to purchase:

Rocking horse
Blocks
Dolls and doll clothing
Musical instruments
Puzzles
Wagon
Housekeeping toys
Toy animals
Puppets
Construction toys (Legos, Tinker Toys, Lincoln Logs, etc.)
Doll houses
Small figures (e.g., families: Mom, Dad, boy and girl children)
Beginning board games (e.g., Candyland, Chutes & Ladders, Hi-Ho Cherry-O)

A Word about War Toys

Many parents and child care providers are concerned today over the issue of buying children war toys (guns, tanks, GI Joes) and allowing war play at home or in child care. Symbols of power or strength are very attractive to young children; they will beg for commercial war toys, or if denied them, will make sticks or fingers into weapons and play anyway.

Many children also enjoy playing "Superheroes." Again, this stems from wanting to feel powerful. The play, however, often incorporates more constructive themes (rescuing those in distress) than typical war play, which always includes shooting or killing. Most providers allow Superhero play but place limits on it (e.g., no weapons).

Some providers ban war toys and war play altogether. Early childhood educator and therapist Susanne Wichert makes this compelling case for disallowing war toys:

- Watching others be aggressive (in cartoons or in books) models aggressive behavior. Children act out what they see.
- Toys that glamorize violence diminish a child's sense of security in the long run. It is irresponsible to give children a view of death that is temporary when the likelihood that death will touch their lives is great.
- When children engage in war play, they tend to become very excited and escalate out of control. This usually results in hurt or angry children.
- Commercial war toys encourage children to limit their play content to the "script" provided by the toy manufacturer.
- If children are treated with respect and feel comfortable about their rate of growth, they have less need to escape into characters who rule others.*

If you do ban war play, it is critical that you provide ample alternative adventure play for the children. You must intervene when violent play emerges and direct the children to other, more appropriate action play.

*From *Keeping the Peace: Practicing Cooperation and Conflict Resolution with Preschoolers,* by Susanne Wichert (Philadelphia: New Society Publishers, 1989).

Find stories with strong adventure themes. *Where the Wild Things Are* by Maurice Sendak is a good adventurous, nonviolent story. For younger children, Helen Oxenbury's version of *We're Going on a Bear Hunt* is also a good choice. Children will act out these themes and stories in their play.

Other providers choose to allow some war play, but impose strict limits. Betsy, a long-time provider, describes her policy:

> We have a few hard and fast rules. 1) No commercial war toys (those bought at toy stores) are allowed here. If children choose to make a sword out of a stick, or use their crackers as "bombs," we do allow that, since it engages their imagination in dramatic play. 2) Absolutely no pointing "guns" or other weapons at people or animals. They can "shoot" at targets or other inanimate objects.

Watch for appropriate dramatic play. Sometimes war play degenerates into just one action (shooting) and the children get into an unending loop of pretend violence. One provider shares how she was able to redirect some inappropriate play:

> Three preschoolers were playing cowboys and bandits. Two children were the cowboys and they insisted the third be the bandit. Jason, the bandit, got tired of being shot all the time and wanted to be a cowboy. The other two refused to switch, and the situation went downhill from there. I intervened, suggesting that they all be cowboys and go on a dangerous mission. "Now what could the dangerous mission be?" I mused. "We could find a wild beast," offered Mason. "Great," I said, "what will the beast be doing?" "He's got some kids!" announced Jason excitedly. "Yeah, and we have to save them," contributed Eric. All three boys went racing off to enact this scenario.

If you do allow war play, make sure the materials you provide encourage children to expand this play and use their imaginations. More learning results from open-ended dramatic play than it does from manipulating a toy that just does one thing (e.g., shoots a missile or fires a dart or "bullet").

Structured Time

Structured time means you choose the activity or play for the children, plan it, and direct it. Examples of structured time include welcoming time, circle time, curriculum themes and activities, TV time, and special events such as holidays, birthdays, and field trips.

Circle Time and Welcoming Time

Circle time is a classic child care activity that can be personalized to fit a curriculum theme for the month, used as a welcoming ritual, or adapted to teach specific skills. Children and provider sit in a circle (usually on mats or carpet squares) for different group activities. You can tell stories, sing songs, have sharing time, and more. Welcoming time uses the circle format to formally welcome and recognize each child. For the children, welcoming time is esteem-building, consistent, and a nice way to start off the day's activities. Here's how a few different providers use circle time and welcoming time.

Karen uses a little song as a welcoming ritual and a self-esteem builder:

Where's Jason? Where, where?
Where's Jason? Where, where?
Where's Jason? Where, where?
There's Jason, there, there. (Whisper this line)
Is he up on the mountain? No, no.
Is he down by the fountain? No, no.
Has he gone out to play? No, no.
I see Jason is here today!
One, two, three! (Child stands up)

Another provider shares her use of circle time:

We generally use circle time as a lead-in to the curriculum activity. One feature is always the same. We start out by acknowledging all the children present with our spelling song:

Caitlyn, Caitlyn, is here today,
She's so special in every way.
Now we'll play the spelling game,
By spelling the letters of her name,
C-A-I-T-L-Y-N!

When we spell, I point each letter out on a name placard I have on the wall. It helps them begin to learn about the alphabet.

Tina uses circle time more casually, tuning into the children's moods and interests that day.

Sometimes we do a lot of Knock-Knock jokes (the three- and four-year-olds love them), sing songs, read books, or have sharing time.

Activity Time

Some providers have a very structured activity time organized into a preschool curriculum and based on a theme. Camille, mentioned above, follows this theme schedule every year:

September: Bugs, insects; "all-about-me" name tag tree (wall display)

October: Fall, Halloween; hang pumpkins on the name tree

November: Farm animals; big leaves on the name tree; field trip to the zoo

December: Holidays (Dutch Santa Claus—make wooden shoes; Swedish Santa Lucia—make wreaths with paper candles; Hanukkah—play dreidel)

January: Transportation, occupations; wall displays with children's names

February: Winter

March: Dinosaurs

April: Wild animals, Noah's Ark display on wall

May: Ocean, water; field trip to Aquarium

Summer months: No set curriculum; outdoor play

It is often useful to plan out the year this way, because you can repeat the program and re-use the materials year after year, thereby dramatically reducing your preparation time. Camille laminates the materials for the wall with either clear contact or self-laminating paper; the materials adhere to the wall with Fun Tac, a putty that will stick to the wall without damaging the paint.

Felt boards are also a good option for a thematic curriculum. You can buy them in "story sets" (for example, all the pieces you need to tell the story of the Three Little Pigs) or in curriculum sets (numbers, letters, farm animals, etc.). Children enjoy watching each piece go up on the board as you teach or tell a story. You can re-use the felt pieces year after year. Use velcro on the backing to help them stick to the board. Camille talks about how the children respond to the felt board:

> The children love the felt board stories even more than TV, if you can believe that. It takes them one or two stories at the beginning of the year to get used to it, but after that, it's clear sailing.

Many providers plan their activities loosely around the seasons. Laurel, for instance, plans art projects according to what holiday is approaching.

> In the fall, we carve pumpkins and make Pilgrim hats. When Christmas nears, we make ornaments for the tree out of shells (children glue in a picture of themselves and sprinkle glitter on it). In the spring, we make Easter baskets and color eggs. And then for Mother's Day and Father's Day, we make decorative soaps for the moms and rock turtles for the dads. For each season, we sing songs about that holiday and decorate the room.

Karen, a provider for special-needs children, plans a theme for each month as she goes along.

> I get ideas for the curriculum from activity books and then I plan activities based on the theme. This month we're learning about sand and the desert. I put up a big cactus cut-out on the board, with prickly-pear blooms with each child's name on it. I read different children's books about the desert and what

lives there. The hands-on activities are generally cooperative and involve sand.

Chapter 5 offers a wide variety of child-tested activity ideas based on the traditional curriculum areas of Language, Science, Learning Games, Movement, Cooking, Music, Art, and Safety.

TV Time: Should You Allow It?

The debate over whether television viewing is ultimately a positive or negative experience for young children is about as passionate as the debate over war toys. Research has found that:

- TV is an excellent teacher of action and dynamic processes (such as how a plant grows) but is less effective at conveying feelings and thoughts.
- TV can teach letters, numbers, concepts, and prereading skills.
- TV promotes aggression. Children's programs are typically more violent than adult programs. Weekend morning cartoons depict twenty to twenty-five violent acts per hour. Children model the aggression they see on TV.
- Heavy TV viewing interferes with educational achievement. Studies show that elementary school-aged children who watch a lot of television do worse in school than their counterparts who watch less television. Preschool children who are heavy viewers engage in less imaginative play.
- TV learning is passive, and it is known that children learn best from interaction.
- TV perpetuates stereotypes. Males outnumber females on TV three to one and are pictured in active, independent, problem-solving roles. Females are predominantly portrayed as deferential, passive, and over 80 percent are portrayed as homemakers (as opposed to the real life statistic of well over 50 percent of adult women in the workplace).

The evidence here is pretty clear: heavy and/or indiscriminate viewing is harmful to children. For this reason, many providers do not allow TV viewing.

Other providers take a more middle-of-the-road approach and allow selected, approved viewing. Laura describes her policy:

> We have a rainy day policy with regard to TV. If we can't play outdoors in the afternoon, children have a choice of watching *Mr. Roger's Neighborhood* or engaging in free play. I will occasionally allow *Sesame Street,* but I don't like them to watch more than one show a day.

An alternative to TV is to offer the children a choice of videos. There are many good videos on the market. Deborah, a provider with a large license, talks about how she handles videos:

> We watch one video a week. I like to let the children bring in their favorite. The videos we've watched in the past few months have included *Barney, Sesame Street, Wee Sing,* and much *Disney.* The only problem I run into is every child wanting to bring in the same movie. I solve this by talking with the parent ahead of time and thereby avoiding 500 screenings of *Beauty and the Beast.*

Be cautious with how much TV you allow children to watch. Once you form your policy on it, stick to it.

Special Events

Experienced providers find it wise to structure special routines or set rules for handling holidays, birthdays, and field trips. Here are a few tips.

Holidays

Children love holidays and the special celebrations that come with them. But unless you're providing care for all your friends from church, it's best to keep holiday celebrations fairly secular or make an attempt to note most of the major religious holidays.

Camille chooses to celebrate the Christmas season by incorporating Dutch and Swedish "Santa" traditions into the activities; she also teaches the children to play the Hanukkah game of dreidel. Tina focuses on the Easter bunny part of the holiday instead of the religious story.

This is not to say that you absolutely cannot include Bible stories or prayer in your child care. But you should be very sensitive to the ethnic and religious traditions of the families you service and structure your holiday celebrations accordingly.

Brenda shares her thoughts on this.

I try to celebrate the holidays that the children observe at home. I have three children who are Mormon, so I always do something for their "Pioneer Day" on July 24th. Last time we dressed up as pioneers and pretended to have a wagon train.

This past fall I had a few moms who were very uncomfortable with Halloween. So instead of making Jack-o-Lanterns, we had a barn party. I decorated the play room with hay and a scarecrow and all the children came in animal or farm costume. They loved it.

Another provider recommends downplaying major religious holidays, like Christmas or Passover, and playing up the secular ones, like George Washington's Birthday.

We do lots of reading about and looking forward to Presidents Day. We read beginning biographies about Washington and Lincoln and talk about who the president is now. Then we make George Washington hats (like the one he wore in the painting crossing the Delaware) out of newspaper and Lincoln top hats out of construction paper. We make cherry tarts for snack. We all have great fun in February.

Birthdays

Young children's birthdays are probably the most exciting day of the year to them. It is very easy, however, for children to become overexcited and overstimulated. Providers find that setting consistent rules on how birthdays are handled helps eliminate any problems. Here are some suggestions.

From Tina:

I ask the parent to bring a low-sugar treat for all the children. Usually it's pink rice-crispie treats or applesauce cupcakes. We sing "Happy Birthday" before we eat the treats.

Camille's birthday routine is more structured and rigid, due to problems she's had:

I was very bothered by the unequal treatment the children received when the treats and favors were left up to the parents. Some parents would go all out—even do too much—and others would practically ignore their child's birthday. So, to even things out, I established my own birthday routine.

I made a special, reusable paper crown that the birthday child gets to wear at mealtimes. The other children wear reusable party hats. After lunch, instead of a cake (many children don't like cake and I find cupcakes too messy) I make a small pyramid out of frozen ice cream sandwiches, cut in half. I put a few candles on top. Sometimes I give them noisemakers (I get them in bulk) to play with or we play a no-lose version of musical chairs (where there are chairs enough for everybody).

When the child leaves that day, I give him a special, small present from me. He's not allowed to open it until he gets home.

Remember, if there are favors or treats, there should be one for everyone. Children three and younger are not really ready for structured games, while fours and fives do better with party games. You can set whatever birthday routines and rules that work best for you.

Field Trips

Getting out of the house occasionally and exploring the world is good for you and the children. There is virtually no end to places that young children will find fascinating. Some common field trip destinations are:

- The zoo
- An indoor children's gym

- A children's museum/science center
- A park or nature preserve with trails for hiking
- An airport
- An aquarium
- A fire station
- Your public library (they often have special storytimes and events).

Karen tells about the time she and her assistants took five four-year-olds to an indoor children's gymnasium.

> I care mostly for children from low-income families. They had never been to such a place. After a few minutes of wide-eyed wonder, they plunged in, sliding, jumping and climbing on the equipment. They talked about it for days.

Always inform parents ahead of time of an upcoming field trip and get permission to take each child. The logistics of finding additional adult escorts and adequate transportation is usually the hardest part of a field trip. There should be, however, a willing volunteer or two from your group of parents to help out. If there is an entrance fee, ask the parents to be responsible for the cost of their child's fee.

In a public place, try to have one adult for every three children. Talk to the children ahead of time about where you are going and what kind of behavior you expect from them. The buddy system, where you assign two children to each other and direct them to hold hands at all times, often works well.

Be creative in the places you take the children. Perhaps you have a friend with a pottery wheel in her garage who is willing to demonstrate for the children. Or maybe the neighbor across the street who works at a bakery would arrange for a tour.

Jan, a provider with a small license and a small budget, shares her novel idea for a field trip.

> I live in the area of Seattle called Fremont. There is a huge bridge nearby. At the top of the hill, underneath the northern corner of the bridge, some local artisans have created an enormous Troll. Its eye is a headlight from a car and it is clutching a real Volkswagen bug in its hand.

First, we read stories about trolls (*The Three Billy Goats Gruff,* and *The Trouble with Trolls,* by Jan Brett). Then I took the children to see the Fremont Troll one day; it was just a short walk from my house. Now it is their favorite field trip destination.

Try also to bring in interesting people occsaionally who can talk about their jobs with the children. Some possibilities are:

- A pilot
- An author
- An artist
- A police officer.

The list could go on and on. Take care to show women and men in a variety of roles—both traditional and nontraditional. One provider had a teenage friend who played football come in and talk to the children. The hook? The teenager was a girl.

Story Time

Make story time a regular part of your day. It's just as important as block play or outdoor play. Few things bring adults and children more fun and intimacy than reading a favorite story together.

There are literally thousands of books published each year for young children. Selecting and buying them can be one of the more fun tasks for your business, and one of the most important. How can you choose well?

Appendix A lists some top picks for individual children's books as well as some suggested mail-order catalogs that sell books for children and adults. What follows are some points to keep in mind when selecting and reading books to young children.

Children get a myriad of benefits from being read to. A few of them are:

- Learning new ideas and words
- A fun chance to sit together as a group, or to sit on a lap with one adult and be cuddled

- Practice at sorting out what is real and what is pretend
- A way to identify with and sort out feelings
- Stimulating imagination
- A chance to participate in a story.

In addition, curriculum activities can include stories or even be structured around them. For example, Sherry, a provider for about two years, shares how she uses books in her curriculum.

> We're doing a unit on "Other Lands." I started with France and have read a variety of books that are set in Paris to the children: *The Cows Are Going to Paris* by David Kirby and Allen Woodman, *Flight* (the story of Charles Lindbergh's historic flight to Paris) by Robert Burleigh, *Madeline* by Ludwig Bemelmans, and *Minou* by Mindy Bingham. Some of the books are too text-heavy for the three-year-olds, so I just abbreviate the story as I go along, focusing mostly on the illustrations. It works well. The children are so excited now if they spot a poster of the Eiffel Tower or see it on TV.

There are many ways you can help children learn to love books (which often translates later into a love of reading) and increase their appreciation of how powerful books can be in their lives. The following is a list of general tips for reading to children and some specific information on reading to children at different ages.

- Always read a book yourself first, before reading it to the children. Be on the lookout for stories that show children as competent problem solvers. Stories that show adults always solving the conflict for children are poor models.
- Willingly read old favorites over to children; avoid an endless stream of new books. Familiarity with a certain story will help children incorporate aspects of it into their dramatic play.
- Take the children to a library or bookstore regularly. Let the children see the "source" of books and the wide variety of them available.
- When children ask a question you don't know the answer to, such as "How many miles is it to Paris?", let them help

you look up the answer. This will show them answers can be found in books.

- Provide a wide variety of books (fiction and nonfiction) for free play in a cozy spot. Encourage children to use the book corner. Although most children can't read text yet, they can look at the pictures. If it goes unused for a while, change the books and go there yourself to read one of them. If children see you reading, they will want to do so too.

- Select books that are not racially or gender biased, and remember that children need to see themselves in stories. Balance your collection of books. A little girl will not identify with an unending parade of boy characters in trucks, nor will a Hispanic child identify with books that show only Caucasian families. Even if you care for just one ethnic group, children live in a richly-varied world; it's good for them to see the differences.

Be aware too, of sexist language lurking in the text. "Policeman" really should be "police officer." Words, however, are more easily altered by you than are pictures. Be on the lookout and do your own editing as you read stories.

Books for Babies

Very young babies like looking at pictures of faces, familiar objects (bottles, shoes, hats, spoons), and other babies. They tend to be more attracted to color photographs rather than drawings, though as they grow older, they will like both.

Find sturdy board books, cloth books, or plastic books that babies can chew on and not destroy. It's okay to chew on a book when you're a baby—it's just another way to explore what a book is and what it does. (Books for babies are made of nontoxic materials. Be sure to wipe them off as the book gets passed around.)

Reading to a baby should last only as long as his interest does. If his attention span is no longer than forty-five seconds, go on to some other activity. As babies near their first birthday, they will begin to choose to play with books, and by about age fifteen months will be helping you turn pages.

Don't be intimidated by books without words. Look at the pictures with the baby, name the objects or action, and see if the child can point to what you name. A sample "dialogue" might go like this: "Look at that. The daddy is feeding the baby. They look cozy, don't they? Let's turn the page. Where's the baby? That's right! There she is." Wordless books are also good choices for preschoolers to "read" with babies. Many four- and five-year-olds enjoy sharing books with their young friends.

Older babies are attracted to simple text with rhymes or a strong rhythm and colorful, familiar illustrations.

Reading with Toddlers

On-the-move toddlers will often settle down surprisingly well for a story. They love reading the same book over and over again, for as long as you have patience. Simple text (not too many words on a page) holds their attention best, and like older babies, they respond eagerly to rhythm, rhyme, and repetition. Nursery rhymes are very popular with this age group. Toddlers also like books about what is familiar in their own lives: going to bed, playing, eating, getting dressed, and so on.

You can still abbreviate text with this age group (although by age two and a half, you may get strong protests if you skip even a word). One provider talks about how she shortened a book for toddlers:

> My toddlers love *Max's Dragon Shirt* by Rosemary Wells. The text is too long for them to sit through, so we just turn the pages looking for the dragon shirt in each picture. "Is it there?" I ask at each page. They respond eagerly, looking forward to the pictures that show the dragon shirt. I also ask them, "How does Max feel?" when the illustration is particularly expressive. They love to see him feeling happy and covered with ice cream at the end of the story.

Reading with Preschoolers

Books continue to be of major interest to preschoolers and happily, their attention span has increased. Books that show aspects of their everyday lives remain popular, but preschoolers are also interested in all sorts of themes and settings they haven't encountered before. They still like to have books read over and over again, and become very upset if you skip anything; many children will memorize the text and recite it or "read" it to themselves later.

Many children develop favorite authors. Andrea shares a story about Dr. Seuss:

> I've got some hard-core Dr. Seuss addicts in my care. They know by the look of the book if it's a Dr. Seuss, but they still ask me to make sure it's written by him. I even get questions about where he lives and what kind of doctor he is.

Preschoolers are receptive to all kinds of books—not just storybooks. Try out children's nonfiction: read books about bugs, trains, or whatever their interest may be. Don't forget beginning biographies ("This book is about a *real* person"), or life-skills books (e.g., personal safety).

A Word about Teaching Young Children to Read

Many providers report parents trying to teach their toddlers and preschoolers to read, or pushing for the provider to do so or support their efforts.

But before they learn to read themselves, children need a solid base of pre-reading language experiences. Being read to is high on the list. It is more important that children have active experience playing and interacting with the world and then be given the opportunity to talk about it than to have formal reading training.

Discourage parents who want their toddlers or preschoolers to learn to read. It is not appropriate for this age. Occasionally, an exceptional or gifted four- or five-year-old may develop reading skills. You can encourage and foster these skills in cooperation with the child's parents.

5

Fun Activities for Children

The activities you do with children are often among the most rewarding aspects of providing family child care. It is gratifying to watch young children become absorbed in the many learning experiences you can provide. Remember, activities done with infants should have your constant and careful supervision, especially when the older children are assisting.

A good mix of activities includes indoor and outdoor play as well as active and quiet play. When planning activities, allow for both provider-initiated play (organized projects and games) and child-initiated activities (free play). Activities should involve a mix of fine motor skills (drawing, using scissors, playing with puzzles) and gross motor skills (running, jumping, climbing) and should also provide frequent opportunities for process-oriented creative play (art, water and sand play, music).

Providers need to be aware of the children's developmental levels and estimate how much time is appropriate for each planned activity. No child should be forced to participate, but neither should he be allowed to wander aimlessly; give him a choice of what he could do while the others participate in the activity.

As you get to know your particular mix of children and become familiar with their levels of development and interests, certain activities will hit you as "right." Some work better with a small group of children and some are geared to large groups. Trust your instincts as you select activities and feel free to adapt them to your group's needs.

Language Activities

Babies have an innate capacity for language. They learn through the "conversations" and games the adults in their lives share with them. Most of us naturally make language interesting for babies; we vary the pitch in our voices, use accompanying dramatic facial expressions, repeat words, ask questions, and react enthusiastically when the baby responds. Babies understand far more than they can express (this is generally true of children of all ages) and benefit from the talking and playing you do with them. Language activities for babies are generally simple and fun for both of you. Crying and cooing are the first sounds babies make. As they grow they begin to babble (also called "jargoning") and then first words begin to appear.

Enormous leaps in language development occur in the toddler and preschool years. During the second year of life, toddlers will make a two-word sentence, give their first and last names, and begin to use plurals. Toddlers' language tends to focus on the here-and-now, and sentences are rarely longer than two or three words. They describe things ("Big truck!"), make requests ("Milk, now!"), and use language to accompany their play (make engine noises as they push a toy train across the floor).

From here on, language development snowballs. Preschoolers comprehend prepositions, talk about the past ("When I was a little baby . . . ") and the future ("My daddy's takin' me to Disneyland in August") as well as the present. They remember and proudly repeat information imparted by adults ("That's a '57 Chevy"). And they eagerly listen to and discuss stories, and mimic reading.

There is no end to the amount of enriching language experiences you can provide for the children. Activities can range from simply having a group conversation or reading a story, to more complicated projects, like making their own books. Here are a few ideas.

Language Activities for Babies

- Babies like to hear you, as well as the other children, talk, sing, or hum. They tend to react to higher-pitched voices more readily—hence their interest in women's and children's speech. Get into the habit of talking to the babies in your care about what you are doing. The sound of your voice will comfort them. As they get older, they will understand more and more of what you are saying. The older children will see and hear you interact this way with the babies and will mimic you.

  You can also sing or hum to the baby. Some well-known songs you might like to try include:
  "Twinkle, Twinkle, Little Star;" "Hush, Little Baby, Don't You Cry;" "Rock-a-Bye Baby;" "Itsy Bitsy Spider;" "I'm a Little Teapot;" "This Old Man;" and "Three Little Monkeys." Many of these have accompanying finger motions the babies will enjoy.
  The nonsense words in nursery rhymes are fun for babies and the rhymes and rhythms will help them learn to listen. Babies like to hear these chants and rhymes over and over again. It's often fun for the older children to join in as well. Try "Pease Porridge Hot;" "Eeeney, Meeney, Miney, Mo;" "Hey, Diddle Diddle;" "Hickory, Dickory Dock;" "This Little Piggy Went to Market;" and "Here's the Church."
  See Appendix for sources of nursery rhymes and fingerplays.
- Even very young babies love books. If they learn that books mean fun time with you and the children, they will look forward to story time. It will help them learn to listen for rhythm and rhyme, and they will like looking at the pictures.
  Choose sturdy board books or cloth books. For suggested titles, see the Appendix. Preschoolers will enjoy "reading"

wordless picture books to the babies. For a more complete discussion of reading to babies, see chapter 4.

Language Activities for Toddlers

- Save the lids that come on cans of frozen juices. Wash and dry them. Sit down with the toddlers and have them choose pictures of people from old magazines. Later, on your own, cut and glue these pictures to one side of the juice lids. (This activity is even more fun if you glue snapshots of the children to the lids.)

  Then, with the children, put the lids on the floor, face down. Take turns picking them up. When a child picks one up, say, "That's the mommy," "That's the baby," or, "That's the daddy." Ask the child to point to the eyes, ears, nose, and so on of each face. Soon, the children will be telling you which person they've picked up and will name the features.

- Toddlers also love books. Suggestions for good ones to read to them can be found in the Appendix. It is also fun for toddlers to make their own books. Look through old magazines and ask the children to select pictures. Cut them out, and then have the children mount the pictures on thin cardboard. Punch the pages with a hole-punch and tie them together with string or yarn. You and the children can make up a story to accompany the book. Remember to follow the child's lead. If he wants to read the pages as "banana day, apple day, pear day," then cooperate and honor his choice. When adults edit children's creations too much, they get the message that what they've done isn't good enough.

  When selecting books for toddlers, look for sturdy books with cardboard pages or made from cloth. Toddlers tend to be rough with pages and dislike dust jackets. Children this age also enjoy books with very few words and rhyming or rhythmic text. Younger toddlers tend to prefer clear photographs. As they get older and with reading experience, they will love colorful drawings.

  When you read with toddlers, feel free to ignore the written text and just talk about the pictures. Or simply abbreviate the text to fit the attention span of the kids at hand.

- Toddlers love to hear the same story over and over again. One fun thing to do is to tape yourself reading a favorite book. Read slowly, with a great deal of expression. As you make the tape, it's helpful to include reminders like, "Turn the page, now." Talk about the pictures ("Boy, he sure did get ice cream all over his shirt, didn't he?"). Then let a few toddlers listen to the tape and "read" the book by themselves.

Language Activities for Preschoolers

- Preschoolers wield their language mightily in dramatic play. With some easily-obtained props, you can facilitate some rich play environments and watch them go at it. For example, create a mock office for preschoolers to play in. Set up some tables and chairs, and small desks, if you have them. Provide the children with a variety of supplies—paper, pencils, felt tip markers, discarded junk mail to open, play telephones, and stickers that look like stamps.

  Children love to play house, too. Many providers already have play kitchens; if you don't, you can easily create one with large boxes. Supply the kitchen with extra plastic dishes, small, rinsed out milk cartons, plastic fruit, anything that is safe to make believe with.

  Provide dolls and cradles (use shoebox beds if you don't have wooden cradles) for added play. One provider showed children how to tie shawls in order to carry babies on their backs, as is done in many other countries. She reports the children (boys and girls) loved this and carried their dolls around with them during play and mealtimes and even tried to nap with them.

  You can also create a space for building forts. It can be as simple as bringing out chairs, blankets, and pillows and letting the children use their imaginations to build a house, pioneer fort, or motor home.

- Books can be used for more than story time. Choose a favorite story the children know well, such as Maurice

Sendak's *Where the Wild Things Are*, Graeme Base's *Jabber-wocky*, or Ludwig Bemelman's *Madeline,* and read it one more time. Then give the children puppets, stuffed animals, or dolls, and have them act out the story.

- Telling stories is a fun way to exercise language and creativity. Have children tell you a story and write it down for them. If necessary, give them a starter line—for example, "Once upon a time there was a little flower growing on the hill . . ."—and let them finish the story.

Be sure to write down the story exactly as the child utters it; do not correct grammar or pronunciation. Then read the stories back to the children in a natural voice. Children will enjoy hearing their own words and feel proud of their creation.

Science Activities

The natural world is an endless source of fascination to young children. Everything is new and fresh to them. They are just learning about cause and effect and they eagerly experiment with just about anything. Take advantage of this curiosity and foster it with fun science and nature activities.

Science Activities for Babies

- Babies learn about the world through sensation. Helping them exercise their sense of smell can be fun for all involved (older children usually enjoy helping with this activity). Try offering babies a mixture of sweet and pungent smells, such as vanilla extract, cinnamon stick, dill pickle, garlic powder, and mild perfume.

Hold the object under his nose (but not too close). Gently move it back and forth. Have the older children watch the baby's face and decide if he likes the smell. If so, say, "You like to smell vanilla." If not, say, "You don't like to smell vanilla" and put it away. If a baby dislikes the smell, don't offer it again.

- Babies enjoy the feel of water. One safe way to facilitate this is to fill a large, Zip-lock freezer bag with water (only about three-quarters full—if you overfill the bag, it could be burst open). Cut out simple shapes from sponges and put them in the water. Letting out any air, firmly seal the bag.

  The babies can pat the bag, feel the texture of water through the plastic, and look at the colorful sponge shapes.

- Babies learn a great deal about the world through their sense of touch. The many tactile experiences they have help their brains develop. Invite the older children to help you as you try the following sensory experiences: While you're changing a baby's diaper, give her a sticker or a piece of tape to play with. Say, "It's sticky, isn't it?" Let her play with it until she loses interest.

  At lunch time, let the baby hold and mouth an ice cube. Say, "Ice is *cold*!"

  After lunch, hold the baby's hands under the faucet. Run some warm water. Say, "This water is *warm*."

Science Activities for Toddlers

- Water play is fun and a wonderful sensory experience for toddlers. The pouring, dumping, and measuring they do helps develop eye-hand coordination and fine motor skills.

  Get a plastic dishpan of water, plenty of towels, and find a good place to play, such as a small table, outdoors, or your open dishwasher door (the water will run into the dishwasher instead of onto the floor).

  Give the children different props to use with the water, such as measuring spoons, funnels, yogurt containers, sponges, and plastic soda bottles cut in half (smooth the cut edges or tape them over with duct tape).

  Remember that whenever children are around water, you need to supervise the play very carefully and ensure safety.

- Simple science experiments are fun for older toddlers. The different seasons lend themselves to different activities. In the summertime, you can fill two small glass jars evenly with water. Put one in a sunny window or outside in the sun. Put the other in a shady, cool spot. Let the children look at the jars a few hours later and see how they compare. Talk about how water evaporates quickly when it's hot.

In the wintertime, have the children make snowballs. Put the snowballs in two baking dishes. Put one dish in the freezer and place the other dish on a counter. After twenty minutes, compare the two dishes. Talk about what makes the snowballs melt.

- Go on a nature walk in your neighborhood or park and look for worms. They like to come out just after rainfall. Or get a spade and dig a little. Let the children gently touch and feel the worms. Talk about how worms get their food from the dirt and enrich the soil.

Science Activities for Preschoolers

- Growing seeds is an engrossing activity for any age, but preschoolers are especially entranced by watching sprouts emerge and the plants grow.

If you have garden space outside, you're in business. Beans and peas germinate and grow the fastest. Squashes, like pumpkin or zucchini, are popular since they grow quite large. Another fun plant is the sunflower. It is large, dramatic, and you can roast and eat the seeds in the fall.

An inside variation on this activity is to "plant" an avocado pit or sweet potato in a jar of water. Stick three toothpicks into the midsection and rest the bottom third in water. Watch the roots grow in the water and leaves sprout on top.

- Preschoolers love to play with magnets. You can extend their learning by providing opportunities for them to explore which objects are attracted to a magnet and which are not.

Make up a shoebox of items that are made of iron and steel (for example, paper clips, keys, crochet hooks, and metal buttons) and then include some nonmetal items (for example, plastic buttons, wooden pencils, crayons, and toothbrushes).

Have the children take turns holding the magnet and choosing something from the box. Talk about why the magnet picked up the object or did not.

Learning Games

This is a broad category, but in general, the best learning games for children include a combination of the following elements:

- They promote problem solving. Good learning games encourage children to think and solve whatever fun problem is at hand.
- They encourage cooperation. Group activities are more fun when there are winners only and no losers. You can accomplish this by offering games that require teamwork toward a common goal.
- They foster self-esteem. When children succeed at a game, they feel good about themselves and confident in their ability to meet challenges.
- They require communication: verbal, nonverbal, or both. Children improve and practice their language skills when they play games—especially cooperative ones.
- They allow children to be physical and become aware of their bodies; children discover what their bodies can do and they learn to be respectful of others' bodies.

Of course, the most important element in learning games is *fun*. The more children enjoy an activity, the more they will participate and learn. Once again, be accepting of any children who choose not to join in; find a safe place for them to observe, but don't force them to play.

Learning Games for Babies

- Babies love faces. Peekaboo, that tried-and-true game that's been around forever, is still as relevant to babies' learning as ever. Peekaboo helps babies learn that something (or someone) still exists, even when they can't see it. It's also one that the older children can play with the babies in your care. Peekaboo can be played by covering your own face or by gently covering the baby's face (with a soft cloth) and then removing it.
  By playing mimic games with the older children (or with

mirrors) you can help babies learn where certain body parts are, as well as concepts such as "on" and "off."

Sit down with the baby in front of a group of two or three older children. Have the older kids put hats on their heads. Say, "The hats are *on* their heads!" Point to the hats. Put a hat on the baby's head. Let him take it off and put it back on. Watch him try to find his head.

- This game is the very start of learning to count. Bring out a six-cup muffin tin and six tennis balls (or whatever safe object you have six of).

  Give the baby the muffin tin. Have a preschooler show her how to place one ball into each hole. Let the children take turns putting the balls in and taking them out.

Learning Games for Toddlers

- Toddlers love to play with balls. You can teach them to roll balls back and forth to each other, toss them in boxes, and catch them. These activities help them develop gross motor skills and eye-hand coordination. The younger ones like the larger, lightweight ones, like beach balls; older toddlers can play with smaller, heavier balls. You can make your own cloth balls out of socks or panty hose. Cut off the toe part and stuff it with the rest of the sock, then stitch it securely closed.

- You don't have to buy expensive wooden puzzles for children. Make simple puzzles out of heavy cardboard. For the youngest toddlers, circles are the easiest shapes to begin with. Using sharp scissors or a knife, cut a circle from the cardboard (make the edges as smooth as you can). Color the circle piece.

  Show the toddlers how to put the circle in and take it out. Let them practice it over and over again. Older or more experienced toddlers can graduate to other shapes. Watch them carefully; if they're not ready for a more complicated puzzle, they can get very frustrated. If this happens, put the new puzzle away and let them practice some more on an old one.

- Block play is the beginning of learning math and science skills. Boys tend to be more drawn to block play than girls, but it's important for all children to get a chance to experiment with and use blocks. This game is cooperative and includes everyone.

  Have the children sit in a circle with a box of blocks in the middle. Go around the circle having the first child put a block down and the others build on it. Keep going around the circle until you've used up all the blocks or the block building falls down.

Learning Games for Preschoolers

- Making a spider web out of string is fun for four or more preschoolers. Sit in a small circle. Have the children take turns rolling a ball of heavy string to a person sitting across the circle. Help them learn how to catch and roll with one hand and hang onto their string ends with the other hand. A web will begin to form. Remind them to hold the string ends tightly so the growing web stays taut.

  This is a good cooperative activity; if all children "hold up their end" a beautiful spider web will emerge. If you have a stuffed animal or puppet spider, it is fun to set it in the middle of the web.
- Balloon play, inside (in a large space) or outside, helps children learn to work together toward a common end. Have the children sit in a circle. Depending on how many children you have, give them one or two balloons. Have one child toss the balloon in the air. All the children are responsible for keeping the balloon in the air—tossing it up when it gets close to the ground. Encourage the children to work together so everyone has a turn. If you like, time how long they can keep it in the air. If they wish to, they can play again and try to beat their own time.
- *Simon Says* is a fun game that helps children learn to listen and follow directions. You can be the leader and then turn the role over to one of the children. Take turns being the leader.

Here are a few starter lines:
Simon says, touch your nose.
Simon says, tug your ear.
Turn around. (Simon didn't say!)
Simon says, hop on one foot.
Simon says, pat your neighbor on the back.
Now pat your head. (Simon didn't say!)

Praise the children when they follow the directions correctly. Smile and laugh if a child does it wrong, but don't exclude her from the game. Just say, "Let's try it again."

Movement Activities

Babies, toddlers, and preschoolers are learning to master their bodies and discovering how much those bodies can do. It's important to provide both structured opportunities for children to move in different ways, and free play in which they can simply run around. These activities make use of the gross motor muscles, are a wonderful way to burn off children's normal energy, and can help children work through their emotions.

Movement Activities for Babies

- Gently touching and moving a young baby's arms and legs helps him begin to learn that he has two sides to his body. Here is a quick activity that you can do during diaper changes.

  Lay baby on his back. Gently touch his palms together over the middle of his body. Bring his toes up to touch his nose. Carefully stretch his arms above his head. Bend his legs at the knee, one after the other, as if he were riding a bicycle.

  Talk about each body part as you move it. For example, "These are your toes. Now they're going to touch your nose."

  Kiss and blow on the baby's tummy and hands. Stick out

your tongue and wiggle it left to right. Some babies will stick out their tongues back at you.

- After you've changed the baby, take a minute or two and pretend the baby is an airplane. Pick her up and hold her firmly around the chest, facing you. Lift her up above your head. Say "Baby goes up!" Lower her down. Say "Baby goes down!"

  Then hold her away from you. Say "Baby goes backward!" Pull her back toward you. Say, "Baby goes forward!" Hold her away from you and turn around. Say, "Baby goes around!"

  This game will help baby's body awareness as you move her around in different directions.

Movement Activities for Toddlers

- Toddlers love to dance, especially with scarves. Collect big, sheer, diaphanous scarves in different colors. (If the scarves are too long or big, tie a knot in the middle; you don't want children tripping on them.) Turn on some classical music with a strong beat, and let the children dance, twirl, and toss the scarves around.

  Scarves are fun to incorporate into other activities too, such as dress-up or building forts.

- Simple jumping can occupy toddlers for a long time. If you can invest in a small indoor trampoline, great. If your budget is smaller, consider getting out an old crib mattress (or you could purchase one at a garage sale). Place it on the floor, cover it with a crib sheet, and let the children jump away.

  Make sure the jumping space is safe. You don't want children tumbling off near sharp edges or corners.

- Make a simple obstacle course for toddlers to follow. You can use a small table to crawl under, a chair to sit on, a bench to crawl over, masking tape on the floor to walk a straight line, a broom to jump over, and a pile of pillows to jump in at the end. Demonstrate the course for them at first. Explain that one child at a time may follow the course.

Movement Activities for Preschoolers

- Have two children stand together on a sturdy, large, hard-cover book. The fun is in balancing together, holding only onto each other. See how long each pair can balance before slipping off the book. Give everyone a few chances to succeed. This is a good activity to practice balance and cooperation.
- Create a caterpillar out of preschoolers. Have them all get down on their hands and knees in a line, then show each child how to grasp the ankles of the child in front of her. The "head" or leader decides where the caterpillar will crawl. Tell the children to try not to let go of each other's ankles so they don't break up the caterpillar. Let children take turns being the head.
- Traditional movement games, such as *Ring Around the Rosy* and *London Bridge Is Falling Down,* are tried-and-true favorites of young children. The nice thing about these games is that children can play them with a group of just three or four. An added bonus is that they are simple enough to include toddlers (whom preschoolers love to direct).

Cooking and Snack Activities

Children love to spend time with you in the kitchen. It takes some careful planning, eagle-eye supervision, and more cleanup, but you can successfully integrate learning and cooking. And the best part is, children love to eat what they make.

A baby's contribution in the kitchen is mostly limited to exploring props and foods, but toddlers and preschoolers will enthusiastically participate in any phase of food preparation you allow them to.

Remember, kids in the kitchen require your constant and careful supervision. Try to limit their participation to safe areas and tasks (keep them away from hot stoves, ovens, and dangerous appliances such as mixers or food processors). Many children are fascinated with knives, so be careful to keep yours well out of reach. Older preschoolers, however, can often be taught to safely use a knife with a rounded, dull point. This, of course, would require your strict supervision.

Kitchen Activities for Babies

- For older babies, pots and pans are not cooking tools but fun puzzles. When a baby learns to put a lid on a pot, he is discovering how shapes fit together. This is an easy way to occupy a baby—and still keep an eye on him—while you are preparing lunch.
- Babies are very interested in how some objects fit inside one another, and they will try to push together some objects that don't fit. Many kitchen items are perfect for this game. You can use measuring spoons on a ring, measuring cups that nest inside of one another, or pots and pans that nest inside of one another.
- Everything that comes within a baby's grasp goes into his mouth. Take advantage of this. Set the baby up in a high chair. (This is a pretty good place for him while you're working on a cooking activity with the older children.) Give him two foods to gnaw on that have opposite tastes. For example, sweet and sour (banana and pickle) or salty and bland (saltine cracker and unsalted cracker). Watch him taste the foods. Which tastes does he prefer?

Cooking Activities for Toddlers

- Make a salad with toddlers. They are champions at ripping and tearing and will eagerly go after a head of lettuce. Give them a big, unbreakable bowl to put the greens in. They can dump in other vegetables you wish to add (precut by you) and mix it all up.
- A simple cooking activity older toddlers can do for themselves is to make their own sandwiches. Spreading peanut butter, tuna fish salad, cream cheese, and other soft spreadables is fun for toddlers. Give them blunt table knives, whole wheat bread, and a choice of fillings.

- Part of learning to cook is learning to use kitchen tools and utensils. Get out the play dough and give the children rolling pins and spatulas for making "bread" and "pancakes."

Cooking Activities for Preschoolers

- Making and eating cookies is high on most preschoolers' lists of favorite things to do. Choose a low- or no-sugar recipe (cookbooks are listed in the Appendix). Preschoolers will learn to measure ingredients, mix and stir, and most fun of all, spoon out cookie dough onto the baking sheet. Young children love to taste the batter. Tell them at the outset that no tasting will be allowed until the baked cookies have cooled. Serve the cookies with milk at lunch or snack time.
- Making butter is a classic preschool cooking activity. Seat the children in a circle. Pour one-third of an inch of heavy cream (do not add salt) into a baby food jar. (Give each child his own.) Shake or roll the jars five to seven minutes (rolling will take longer). Sing songs while you shake the jars. You can also talk about the cream's appearance and texture: a heavy creamy liquid, then a lumpy, swishy mixture, and finally, a watery liquid and a lump of butter.

  At snack time, have the children spread the butter on banana bread or crackers.
- Buy several different types of pasta: elbow macaroni, shells, spirals, wheels, bow ties. Put all the pasta shapes in a big bowl in the middle of the table. Have the children sort the pasta by type (muffin tins work well for this). Then have them choose which types of pasta they want included for lunch.

  Note: Scrupulously clean hands are important in this activity.

Music Activities

It's a rare child who doesn't enjoy some kind of music. There are lots of fun ways to incorporate music into learning games and to incorporate learning into music.

Babies are learning to distinguish different sounds, rhythm, and rhyme. Toddlers and preschoolers are beginning to sing and move to music, and to make music themselves. Now is a wonderful time to expose young children to different types of music and to encourage them to create their own.

Music Activities for Babies

- Drums are a fun way to make music or just plain old noise. Tape or glue the lid back onto an empty oatmeal box. It will make a very nice drum. Babies love to make sounds when they hit the drum with their hands or spoons.

    A good time for drum play is when the older children are making music as well; the babies will mimic them.
- Babies love lullabies. At naptime a very natural music activity with babies is to sing to them (or play a tape of quiet songs). Try any of the following: "Twinkle, Twinkle, Little Star;" "Hush, Little Baby;" "Rock-a-bye Baby;" and "Lullaby, and Good Night."
    See Appendix for resources.
- One way babies learn about their world is by listening to the different sounds around them: voices, music, water running, bells ringing, and much more. The daily sounds you and the other children make are interesting to babies. Watch their faces to see which kinds they like.

    Hang a windchime near the baby, low enough that a young child can reach it. Every time you approach, tinkle it gently. Allow the children to ring it occasionally. Watch the baby turn her head toward the sound.

Music Activities for Toddlers

- Toddlers are born mimics and love songs that include movement or finger plays. The following are tried-and-true toddler favorites: "The Itsy-Bitsy Spider;" "I'm a Little Teapot;" and "If You're Happy and You Know It."
    See Appendix for source books on songs and finger plays.
- Bring out a full-length mirror. Find an upbeat song on the

radio, or play a tape you like. Line the children up and have them dance in front of the mirror. Call out a few directions, like, "Dance high! Touch the ceiling!" or, "Dance low, like a snake." Have the children take turns in front of the mirror.

- It's fun to bring out some "jingle bells" and tie them to toddlers' shoes. When you turn on some music, they can make their bells ring as they dance. This is especially fun to do as the holidays approach.

Music Activities for Preschoolers

- Collect some good children's music to listen to, dance to, and sing along with. Some good children's artists are:

  Joanie Bartels—*Morningtime Magic, Sillytime Magic, Dancetime Magic* (Discovery Music)

  Lois Lafond—*I Am Who I Am* (Lois Lafond & Co.)

  Marcia Berman—*Rabbits Dance and Other Songs for Children* (Learning Through Movement)

  Raffi—*Singable Songs for the Very Young; The Corner Grocery Store; Evergreen, Everblue* (MCA Records)

  Dennis Hysom—*The Wooley Cat's Favorite Nursery Rhymes* (Discovery Music)

  Tom Hunter—*Windows* (The Song Growing Co.)

  Miss Jackie—*Sniggles, Squirrels, & Chicken Pox* (Miss Jackie Music Co.)

  Prokofiev—*Peter and the Wolf: A Musical Tale for Children,* narrated by Dudley Moore (Philips Classics)

  There are many more. See your local librarian or bookseller for more suggestions.

- Have the children make their own instruments and create their own band. (Toddlers will enjoy playing these instruments, too.) Here are a few ideas for instruments:

  - A drum made from an oatmeal box.
  - A banjo made from a shoebox. (Tape the lid on. Cut a hole in the top. String three rubber bands across the hole. (Tape a paper towel tube to the side end of the box for a handle.)
  - Rattles and shakers made by putting beans, rice, or pop-

corn into tightly-sealed plastic containers, clean yogurt containers, or clean plastic soda bottles.

- A set of cymbals made by crashing two pot lids together.
- A horn made with a paper towel or toilet paper tube. Punch a few holes in the sides and then cover one end with waxed paper (secure it with a rubber band). Blow and hum through the open end.
- Play Musical Statues. Choose a lively song to play on the radio, or select a tape. While the music is playing, the children dance. When you turn the music off, the children must freeze in whatever position they are in, then stay still and quiet until the music starts again.

Vary the music you choose, from upbeat songs to rap to slow, soothing tunes.

Art Activities

Creativity takes many forms and art projects are one of the best ways to exercise it, no matter what the age. Early childhood educators agree that what is important for young children is the *process* of creating art, not the product itself.

Young children learn by "doing." More learning about creativity takes place in the act of creation than in the finished product. For example, the mushing, squishing, and pounding of clay is more valuable to the child's creative growth than is the "dinosaur" it turns out to be.

Along with messy, process-oriented art, it is also fun to mix in some traditional structured art projects, such as construction-paper flags on Flag Day.

Here are a few tips to help children enjoy creating artwork:

- Never, never draw on, finish, or touch up a child's artwork. Anything he makes is already good enough.
- When you talk with children about their artwork, do not focus on content. Instead of asking, "What's this a picture of?" describe what you see; for example, "I see bright red

circles with three yellow lines going through this one." Another good conversation starter is, "Tell me about your picture/sculpture."

- Be sincere with your praise. Children know when you're blowing something out of proportion, for example, "That's the best picture I ever saw." Instead, be specific about what it is you like; for example, "I like the soft green color you used in the sky part of the picture," or, "I can see you spent a lot of time poking holes over here."

- Occasionally children want to tear up their artwork. Sometimes they just get frustrated trying to achieve a certain effect and sometimes they are simply finished with the picture and don't want it anymore. Respect what they want; the artwork is their creation and they have a right to keep, display, or dispose of it.

- Remember, unless you're making structured art with a set product expected, keep your involvement minimal; children will learn more that way.

- Pay particular attention to safety when you're making art. Choose products that are non-toxic, washable, and safe for children to create with. Supervise them carefully.

Art Activities for Babies

- Young babies like to see simple pictures of people's faces. Their favorite part of the picture is the eyes.

   Using either a thick black felt pen or brightly colored marker, draw a simple, bold picture of a Mommy face on one piece of white paper. Draw a picture of a Daddy face on another piece of white paper. Glue these pictures onto two pieces of cardboard. Cover with clear contact paper.

   Enlist the older children's help in taping one picture to the inside of the baby's playpen or crib for her to look at. With very young babies (ages newborn to six months) make sure the picture is placed down low on the inside of the crib. If she turns her head to the side, she should be able to see the picture no more than 12 inches away.

   After one week, change to the other picture. Babies like

simple patterns too, like bull's-eyes and checkerboards. You can also tape these designs inside the crib.

- A "touchy-feely" board is a sensory toy that helps babies learn about colors, shapes, and textures. It is fairly easy to make and can easily be a cooperative project that involves the older children. You will need several brightly colored fabric scraps of different textures. Some good fabrics are velvet or velveteen, dotted swiss, brocade, carpet scraps, satin, wool, corduroy, terry cloth, fake fur, and quilted fabric.

  Cut out 5-inch squares of material. Glue them onto cardboard in rows of three or four.

  Let the baby feel one square at a time. Watch and see which ones he likes to feel the most. The older children will enjoy watching the baby play with their creation.

- The faces babies are most familiar with are family members', but they should also know the faces in your day care well—and their names. This is a fun project for the older children to help make and a fun game for the baby to show off his skill at identifying faces he knows.

  Gather together an empty, washed milk carton, some newspaper, clear contact paper, glue, and photos of yourself and the children in care.

  Cut the milk carton in half, 5 inches or so from the bottom. Stuff one half with newspaper. Push the two halves together to form a cube.

  Glue pictures of yourself and the children onto each side. Cover the cube with clear contact paper.

  Rotate the cube and show the baby the pictures. If he is old enough to point, ask him to point out you and each of the children pictured. For fun, point to yourself and ask, "Is this Jason?" The baby will enjoy the joke.

Art Activities for Toddlers

- A classic introduction to painting is to give toddlers a bucket of water and some wide paint brushes and have them "paint" your fence or even the side of your house. You will be amazed at how long this will hold their attention. Talk about the brush strokes they are making and how the water makes things look dark.

- Older toddlers like to make collages. Put a handful of each of the following items in a muffin tin: sequins, dry beans, cinnamon, sand, small discarded buttons, elbow macaroni, potpourri, or anything else that might be fun to stick down.

   Give each child a square of clear contact paper, sticky side up. Show them how to sprinkle items onto the sticky surface. When they are done with their designs, cover the collage with another piece of contact paper, sticky side down. This will seal the artwork and preserve it.

- Toddlers are tactile creatures and like to know how things feel. Paint is no exception. Fingerpainting allows them to explore the medium of paint while they create pictures. Use washable tempera paint (available in craft stores and some toy stores) in shallow containers. Provide primary colors (red, yellow, blue) for them to combine to make other colors. Have some water available for them to wash their hands before trying another color. Provide large pieces of butcher paper to paint on.

   Do this activity outside (near a hose for clean-up) or inside on lots of newspapers. Old adult-sized T-shirts make good smocks for children to wear over their clothes.

Art Activities for Preschoolers

- Preschoolers love to make dough, goop, and other kinds of clay. The following recipe makes "Fun Pucky," which is similar to Silly Putty but has its own consistency and color.

   Mix together in one bowl: 2 cups Elmers School Glue and 1 cup water.

   In another bowl mix together: 1 tablespoon Borax and 1 cup water.

   Pour the two mixtures together and watch them react to form Fun Pucky. Mix it with your hands until it's dry enough to play with.

   Give each of the children a piece to explore and mold. Fun Pucky will keep a week or so in a Zip-lock bag.

- Painting is more fun if you explore color-mixing first. Make this a group activity and have the children gather around. One child chooses a primary color and generously dabs it on the paper with a thick paintbrush. Another child chooses a color to add. What color results? Do this again and again. Let the children start to do their own, individual color mixing. Don't be discouraged if they consistently make a muddy brown color—this is how they learn.
- Printing with different objects is an engrossing art activity for preschoolers. Give them some tempera paint and heavy paper, and then provide a wide variety of objects in different shapes.

  Some fun objects to print with are potato pieces, apple pieces, small balloons partially filled with water, sponges, corncobs, or plastic berry baskets (from the produce department of your grocery store).

Personal Safety Activities

Teaching children skills to keep them safe is as important as any other activity you will do with the children. Recent studies have revealed some frightening statistics. We now know that three out of every five girls and two out of every five boys will be sexually molested before they reach age eighteen. Nine out of ten times the abuser is known by the child. As a child care provider you are mandated by the government to report any suspected or observed child abuse or neglect. Some states require you to give handouts to the parents with information on abuse prevention and statistics. You can go beyond these requirements and do even better for the children. You can work with them to build their personal safety skills. (Statistics from the National Committee for Prevention of Child Abuse.)

This section focuses on increasing children's self-esteem, identifying and expressing feelings, building body awareness, and increasing decision-making skills—all things that help protect children from potential abuse.

Many adults are hesitant about teaching personal safety skills to children, fearing that the information will scare them. Research has shown, however, that the informed child is the safer child. Abuse prevention will not scare children if it is presented matter-of-factly and is appropriate for the child's developmental level.

The following activity suggestions are all child-tested and serve to educate and protect children. Note: This is a sensitive topic and you would do well to let parents know when you present personal safety activities. You might send a note home describing the activities and encouraging parents to reinforce the safety information at home.

Personal Safety Activities for Babies

- Part of an infant's job is to learn where her body ends and the rest of the world begins. She is exploring her body and finding out what it can do. This is the time adults and older children can start practicing respect for a baby's body. This means watching her carefully to see what kinds of touching she likes and what kinds she doesn't like or is overstimulated by. Asking questions of the older children will teach them to be sensitive to the baby's needs and likes. Some questions you might try: When you pat or kiss the baby, what does her face look like? How do you think she feels?; If a baby is uncomfortable, how does she let us know? (Emphasize body language here—does the baby cry, fuss, kick, or turn her head away?); and if a baby doesn't like something that she really needs (like having her diaper changed), how can we make it more pleasant for her?

- Everyone has feelings. Babies watch you and the older children express feelings of happiness, sadness, frustration, or pride every day. You can start to give babies words for simple feelings. And you can help them learn that people's faces show what they feel.

    Draw simple faces on paper showing the feelings: happy, sad, surprised, excited, or angry.

    Have the older children help you glue the pictures onto a

large piece of cardboard. Set it up where the baby can see it. Say, "Let's make a happy face." Point to the happy face on the board. You and the older children make happy faces and grin at the baby. Prompt him to look at you and the children and then at the picture.

Repeat with the other pictures. See if the baby will copy you.

- Fostering good self-esteem begins at birth. You can foster babies' emotional health by providing affirmations, that is, positive statements that encourage them to grow. Developmentally, babies need consistent affirmations, even though they don't always understand every word being said. There are two kinds of affirmations we all need—1) for being and 2) for doing. We need to be affirmed for who we are, and for what we can do. Some sample affirmations for babies are as follows:
  - I like you. (being)
  - Your needs are okay with me; I will take care of you. (being)
  - What a terrific smile you have! (being)
  - Wow, you can cry really, really loud! (doing)
  - Look at that, you can sit up all by yourself! (doing)
  - I like the way you explore these toys. (doing)

  Affirmations are appropriate with all ages. You need them as much as the children do. The Appendix lists some resources by educator and author Jean Illsley Clarke that will give you lots of information, props, and ideas on how to make affirmation-giving a natural part of your day for all the age groups present.

Personal Safety Activities for Toddlers

- Establish a Touching Code for your child care. Begin to teach this to children beginning at one year of age. Make the rule simple, such as: Everyone must touch gently; no hurting allowed. Or, if someone is touching you in a way that makes you uncomfortable, say, "Don't touch me! I don't like it!"

  Then enforce the rule. If a child says, "Don't touch me! I

don't like it!" to another, then the other child *must* stop. It's important that everyone follow this rule (including the adults); if you enforce it only occasionally, then children will conclude that you don't really mean it.

If, when restraining a child, you find he tries to use the code on you to get you to let him go, just say, "There is no hurting allowed here. I can't let you hurt yourself or anyone else. I'll keep you safe until you're ready to be calm."

- Practice decision-making skills with toddlers. There's not a whole lot in their lives they are able to control (going to child care, having a bath, etc.) but there are a myriad of small decisions it is appropriate to give them control over. Whenever possible, offer them a choice. For example: Would you like to sit on the green or the red mat? Would you like to take a nap or just rest quietly? Which doll would you like to play with? Would you like to play with the construction toys or make art with the rest of us?

- Read the book *Loving Touches* by Lory Freeman (Parenting Press) with the older toddlers. Talk about what loving touches are and why we need them. Practice giving each other different kinds of loving touches. (Remind the children that anyone who doesn't wish to be touched has a right to use the Touching Code.) Usually, a flurry of big hugs will result.

Personal Safety Activities for Preschoolers

- Read the book *It's MY Body* by Lory Freeman (Parenting Press) with the children. They will enjoy practicing saying, "No, don't touch me. It's *my* body" and "No, I won't touch you. I don't like it."

Then have the children practice the "Safety Yell." Explain that if someone is bothering them, trying to touch them in a way that's uncomfortable, or trying to get them to go with him without a parent's knowledge, then they need to use the Safety Yell and run away. Have the children practice looking you straight in the eye and then yelling as loud as they can (good words to yell: *NO! Mommy! Daddy! Stop it!*). Then have them run to the other side of the room. (*Note:* Some children may giggle or think this is a silly activity. Don't allow any giggling and have the children practice yelling until they produce a good, strong yell.)

Next, present some "What would you do if . . . ?" scenarios. Here are a few sample situations: "What would you do if a big kid took your toy car away from you and said he was going to keep it?" (You could say, "No! It's not yours!" in a loud voice, or find a grownup to help.)

"What would you do if your aunt wanted to kiss you goodbye and you didn't want her to?" (You could say, "No, I don't want to," and shake her hand instead.)

"What would you do if a man stopped his car and offered to give you a puppy?" (You could yell, "NO! in a loud voice, run away, and then tell a grownup.)

"What would you do if your sister were tickling you and you didn't like it?" (You could say, "Don't touch me, I don't like it!" or call a grownup for help.)

"What would you do if you lost your mom in the grocery store?" (You could find a clerk or ask a woman with small children for help.)

Children are more likely to react safely in dangerous situations if they've been taught what to do and have practiced doing it. This activity is a good one to repeat several times throughout the year.

- A critical part of abuse prevention is teaching children to tell the difference between secrets that are hurtful and secrets that are fun surprises. If they can do this, then they will be able to decide when to keep and when to share a secret.

  First read the book *The Trouble with Secrets* by Karen Johnsen (Parenting Press). It presents several situations in which preschoolers are commonly asked to keep a "secret"; for example, a bird's nest no one should know about, a sibling's birthday presents, the hiding place for your house key, and secret passwords. The book also covers scarier situations where keeping a secret isn't appropriate; for example, someone hurts you and warns you not to tell, or maybe one parent tells you not to tell your other parent something.

Make very clear to children that the way you decide to keep or share a secret is by thinking about how the secret makes you feel inside. If it's fun and exciting, like a surprise birthday party, then it's okay to keep. If it hurts or worries you, like uncomfortable touching, then you need to tell a safe person (see below). Encourage children to talk about the secrets they've kept and shared in the past.

Second, have the children draw pictures of at least three or four safe adults in their lives. A safe adult is someone you can tell a scary secret to. Possibilities include parents, you—the child care provider, grandparents, close neighbors, Sunday school teachers, and so on. When they're finished drawing, you should label each picture with the safe adult's name. Emphasize that if the child has a scary secret to tell, and the first person she tells doesn't listen, then she must keep on going down the list. The children should learn to keep telling until they find someone who will listen.

Send the drawings home with the children, and explain to the parents what their purpose is.

- Identifying and talking about feelings is valuable on many levels. When it comes to personal safety, the child who is able to recognize her own feelings of discomfort and warning is not likely to mistake abusive overtures as friendship or caring.

Start by identifying the feelings the children may be experiencing. For example: "Jason fell down. He feels hurt and sad." "When people ignore what I say, I feel frustrated." "Look at Amanda jump for joy. She's really excited." "Boy, I can see that you're really mad we're not going to watch *Sesame Street* today." "You feel happy when your mom comes to pick you up."

Draw some expressive faces on paper or cardboard. Make happy, sad, scared, excited, surprised, mad, and proud faces. During circle time, lay them all face down. Have the children each pick one up and name the feeling.

See Appendix for a more extensive list of recommended resource books for providers and teachers.

6

Positive Guidance Tools

Caring for children is both rewarding and wearing. Part of the frustration and weariness can come from dealing with conflicts between you and the children (No! I won't take a nap!) and conflicts between the children (I had it first! She hit me!).

If you have children of your own, or you've worked with them before, then you know that no one guidance method works with every child all of the time. The reason for this is that at any given time, many, many things contribute to a child's uncooperative behavior:

- The child's developmental stage.
- The match of child and caregiver in temperament.
- Circumstances in the child's day/life (being overtired, sick, etc.).
- Inconsistent or differing rules and expectations at home and in child care.
- Disparity between the child's ability and the caregiver's expectation.
- Desire for attention.
- Experiences in the child's life (new sibling, divorce, illness in the family, and so on).
  This chapter offers you some basic, child-tested guidance

tools. Some of them will seem like common sense to you, while others may elicit an "Ah ha! Why didn't I think of that?" Millions of experienced and loving parents and educators have grappled with this problem before you—and many of them have written about it.

Children's Developmental Ages and Stages

Tremendous growth and development goes on in a child's first five years of life—more so than in any other time in the life span. Nothing will help you more in keeping the children in your care safe and happy than a solid familiarity with children's "ages and stages," that is, the developmental phases all children pass through during the first years of life. There are many areas of development (physical, emotional, social, cognitive, etc.) and all are in interplay at any given time.

Sandy, a first-year provider, talks about how knowledge of development makes a difference.

> When I first started doing child care I was a new mother. My baby was three months old and not giving me much trouble (apart from sleep deprivation!). I began caring for a couple of two-year-olds and instantly had my hands full. Every five minutes there would be a fight over a toy. Mitchell would scream "Mine!" and protect his dinosaur from Katie, who would then beat on Mitchell to try and get the dinosaur. I was ready to strangle them both trying to get them to share. In desperation, I picked up a guidance book on toddlers. Lo and behold, I found that developmentally, toddlers do not yet have the skills necessary to share on a regular basis. I changed my tactics and now I don't put out any especially attractive toys unless there are two of them. When they get closer to three, I'll introduce sharing again.

A good knowledge of development will also help you in planning age-appropriate activities for children, thus avoiding unnecessary frustration on their part and the accompanying headaches for you. The following is a brief chart of the characteristics of the stages of development for children ages newborn to five. Keep in mind that every child is unique; no child will fit nicely into every category. A child who talks early may walk late and be average in other categories. There is no one right age for any developmental milestone, only an age range of what is considered typical—one educator calls this "the wide range of normal."

The characteristics given for different ages are by no means complete. I would strongly encourage you to read books, magazines, and take classes on children's development. The more you know, the easier caring for young children will be on you and them.

Birth to six months
Sets own schedule (sleeping, eating, etc.)
Listens to sounds and voices—particularly parents' voices
Reaches for, bats at, and grasps objects
Imitates actions and sounds
Stares at bright colors
Rolls over, sits with support
Begins to develop eye-hand coordination

Six to twelve months
Sits alone
Babbles
Creeps and crawls
Knows the difference between a strange and a familiar face
Knows own name
Learns by watching others
Uses fingers and thumbs

Knows that objects still exist, even when they can't be seen
Is sometimes frightened of strangers
Plays simple games
Puts everything in the mouth

Twelve to eighteen months
Shows wants without crying
Drinks well from a cup
Responds to spoken requests
Initiates action on own
Plays alone
Scribbles on own
Crawls down stairs backwards
Walks
Manipulates objects
Solves simple problems
May strongly prefer mother
Builds tower of two blocks
Uses simple words, names
Increased awareness of own body

Eighteen to twenty-four months

Takes off clothes
Likes to explore
Makes believe in play
Utters two-word sentences
Mimics family
Names many objects
Builds tower of four blocks
Runs and climbs
Kicks ball
Can point to named body parts
Tests and resists rules
Knows what he or she wants, but can't always express it
Easily frustrated
Often aggressive
Short attention span
Likes to have choices offered
Begins to learn to sing
Plays alongside other children

Two years old

Puts on loose-fitting clothes
Begins to follow rules
Uses short sentences
Builds tower of eight blocks
Tosses ball overhead
Tremendous curiosity and desire to explore
Can solve problems
Begins to separate by saying "No!" a lot
Pedals tricycle
Enjoys showing off strength and daring
Copies drawings

Gives first and last name
Uses plurals
Displays sense of humor
Often very persistent and determined
Protects toys from other children

Three years old

Likes routines
Dresses with supervision
Separates more easily from mother
Usually toilet trained
Learns colors and numbers
Can balance on one foot
Understands prepositions (behind, under, over, etc.)
Likes playing with one or two friends
Starts to understand concept of time
Is now able to share
Drawing becomes more representative of actual objects
Begins to play cooperatively with friends
Enjoys imaginative play
Can make multiple-word sentences
May have nightmares

Four years old

Dresses without supervision
Gives up nap
Draws person with three parts
Hops on one foot
Talks well and frequently

Catches bounced ball
Understands time better
Interested in body parts and gender differences
Enjoys creative projects
May name artwork or creations
Brags
Plays cooperatively with friends

Five years old
Draws person with six parts

Enjoys and needs playtime with friends of own age
Likes organized games
Insists on following rules when playing
Skips
Plans own play and activities
Knows the alphabet
Counts to ten
Needs to feel respected
Likes true stories
Interested in death and what it means

Discipline/Guidance Techniques

Part of being a young child means finding out where the limits are. Setting a "limit" is another way of saying "drawing the line" with regard to children's unacceptable behavior. It is developmentally normal for young children to test your rules and limits again and again in order to see if they are still enforced. Children vary in how much testing they do. The more consistent you are, the faster they will learn, for example, that "people are not for hitting," "food is not for throwing," or, "flower beds are not for stomping."

But some days, even consistency doesn't seem to work. The key to minimizing misbehavior is having lots of options open to you. This section will cover communication and attention techniques, teaching consequences, and fostering good social skills in children. These techniques will stand you in good stead in many, many situations, but it's up to you to choose the tool and follow through. If one technique does not work, try another.

Communication Techniques that Help Children Behave

Shouting "No! Don't do that!" seems to come naturally to most adults who care for children. The trouble is, although it may stop the misbehavior, it doesn't keep it from happening again. Here are three techniques that address problems and help keep them from recurring.

Active Listening

Children usually have their own reasons for what they do, and some feeling behind it. Let's say an eighteen-month-old child begs for milk and then, when she gets it, decides she wants grape juice instead (like her friend). You refuse and she tosses the milk on the carpet.

In this case, the child loves milk, but gets distracted by her friend's juice. It's a much prettier color than her milk. When she demands juice and you set a limit and insist she keep her milk, she gets angry and dumps the milk.

Your response might be to remind her of the rule, "Milk is for drinking, not for spilling." And then you might acknowledge the feelings involved, "When someone spills milk on my carpet, I feel very mad because I have to clean it up" (your feelings); or, "Boy, you feel real mad that you can't have juice. But remember, milk is for drinking, not for spilling" (her feelings).

You can use active listening even with a preverbal child. It consists of noticing what the child is feeling and reflecting it back to him. No questions are asked and no solutions are offered. This is easiest to do when the child's feeling is intense, like anger or frustration, and harder to remember when the behavior is positive, such as curling up with a book (contentment), or jumping for joy (happiness). Here are a few examples of providers using active listening.

> Cassie, age three, and Michelle, age three and a half, were painting pictures. Michelle got upset when Cassie wouldn't share the blue paint. She began to whine and hit Cassie's picture with her brush. Cassie responded by coming to me crying. "Looks like there's a problem here," I said. I looked at Cassie, "It's disappointing when someone splashes paint on your picture." Then I said to Michelle, "You feel mad when Cassie won't share the paint. Hmmm, what can we do here?" Without any input from me, they decided they would each put a lit-

tle blue paint in their own baby food jars to use. It was amazing to me how they calmed down when I talked about their feelings. I think it freed them up to solve the problem.

Joshua is fairly new in my child care. Although it's normal for kids to cry a lot during the first two weeks when their parents leave, this two-and-a-half-year-old seemed more distressed than usual when his mom dropped him off. One day I rocked him for a few minutes and said, "You feel really, really sad to say goodbye to your mommy today, don't you?" He looked up at me, cried a bit more, and then in about five minutes, got off my lap and went to look at the block tower the other kids were making.

Debbie, an experienced provider who has already raised her own family, often has younger parents asking her for advice.

I had a mom ask me about a problem she was having with her three-year-old daughter. She and her husband had recently separated and Sarah was acting out quite a bit. Mom and Sarah were having a power struggle over Sarah's going to bed. Mom picked her up, struggling, and put her in bed. Sarah bounced back up and announced, "I'm going to get a gun and shoot you!" The mom was horrified. I told her for this age, unfortunately, comments like that are pretty typical. Three-year-olds are very impressed with power and the symbols for it. I recommended that she ignore the gun specifics and respond to the feeling Sarah was expressing. Mom decided that next time something like that happened, she would calmly say, "Boy, you're really mad at me right now."

Children really do respond well to having their feelings identified for them. If you know how you feel, you can better decide what to do about it. Children don't always have words for what they feel, so if adults are accustomed to naming feelings for them they will become more at home with their emotions, make better decisions about how to act, and become more sensitive to others' feelings.

You will be communicating that *all* feelings are okay to have, and that limits are placed on how we express those feelings (for example, being mad is okay, but hitting is not). Active listening works best as a prevention tool. You'll find it most effective when the child has a problem, rather than when you have a problem with the child's behavior.

Try to make active listening a regular way of relating to the children. This means reflecting feelings in ordinary, non-conflict situations as well as the more emotionally charged situations. Here are a few examples:

> *You look so cozy and contented when we read stories together.*
> (To an infant) *You're crying because you feel hungry.*
> *You feel excited when we talk about Santa Claus coming.*
> *Daniel feels happy when he talks about his dad coming to see him this weekend.*
> *Wow, look at that block tower you made! I'll bet you feel proud.*

Active listening is just a matter of noticing a feeling and matter-of-factly mentioning it to the children. You don't have to ask questions, tell the child what to do, or solve the problem for her. Often, just reflecting the feeling is enough for the child to come to a resolution (There, somebody understands how I feel!) or to solve the problem herself (like Cassie and Michelle did in the example above).

One word of caution: When talking about feelings, try to avoid the phrase "makes you feel" or "makes me feel." We're all responsible for our own feelings and actions. For example, when you say "Amanda made you mad when she took the doll away," you imply that her feelings can be manipulated by others. What would work better would be a response like, "Amanda took your doll away. You feel mad." Skip the "makes me" or "makes you" part and go straight to "I feel" or "You feel." This slight change in response implies more strongly that the child is responsible for her own feelings.

I-Messages

After you have active listening down, start to practice I-messages. Remember the example of the toddler who spilled his milk on the carpet? When the provider said, "When someone spills milk on my carpet, I feel very mad because I have to clean it up" she was using an I-message.

These statements have three parts:

- *When* . . . (describes in a non-judgmental way the offending behavior)
- *I feel* . . . (describes your feeling)
- *Because* . . . (gives the effect the behavior has on you or others)

Here are a few examples of effective I-messages:
When *you won't stay in your car seat,* I feel *scared* because *I know you're not safe without your seat belt.*
When *children don't help pick up toys,* I feel *tired and frustrated* because *I'll have to pick them up myself.*
When *you interrupt the sharing time,* I feel *mad* because *then no one else gets a turn.*

I-messages clarify a problem situation for children. Oddly enough, many children know when a behavior will irritate a parent or caregiver, but don't know why. An effective I-message will help them understand why the behavior isn't okay. It will also model for children how you take responsibility for your own feelings.

Pay particular attention to the "when" portion of the I-message. Do not use blameful language or generalize overly much. For example, "When you act obnoxious, I feel mad because it isn't respectful" is simply name-calling because it doesn't let the child know exactly *what* she did that you don't like.

A Better Way

This technique, developed by Dr. Haim Ginot, is especially effective with preschoolers, whose language skills have developed enough so they can negotiate with you. (Indeed, some preschoolers' language ability is so skilled, you wonder if you're dealing with a small version of a lawyer or car salesperson!) It is most useful if you use this technique to avoid a power struggle.

There are three parts to A Better Way: 1) state what the

child wants; 2) state what you want; then, 3) ask the child to come up with a better idea that works for both of you.

Lisa recounts one successful use of this technique.

> I wanted Chelsea, age three, to finish her lunch. She had refused her morning snack and her mom reported that she wouldn't eat much breakfast. She had a cheese stick and half a sandwich left to eat. She had heard me use "A Better Way" with the older kids, so I decided to use it on her. "Chelsea," I said, "your way is not to finish your lunch. My way is for you to eat it all up. What's a better way?" Chelsea thought about it and then suggested, "I eat two cheese sticks?" I was delighted with this solution and Chelsea happily ate up two cheese sticks.

A Better Way works only when the child is clear on the fact that the suggestion must be something you *both* like. If a child suggests something that is reasonable, but impractical, try to incorporate as much of that suggestion as possible. For example:

Provider: *Your way is to stay up and play. My way is for you to take a nap now. What's a better way?*
Child: *Mommy sing me a song, first.*
Provider: *Your mom won't be here till three o'clock. I could sing you a song or Cecilia (assistant) could sing you a song.*
Child: *Cecilia needs to sing,* Twinkle, Twinkle, Little Star.
Provider: *That's fine. Let's ask her if she will.*

A Better Way is a simple form of problem solving. It allows the child some control in the situation, avoids an all-out power struggle, and teaches her simple negotiating skills.

Increasing Good Behavior

Believe it or not, "catching them when they're being good" is far more effective than disciplining them when they're misbehaving.

This section looks at three useful ways to notice, compliment, and positively reinforce children when they're behaving well.

Praise

Praising children effectively is based on learning theory that says we *learn* to behave the way we do. Praise reinforces the behavior that immediately precedes it. The best thing about praise is that it's always available; it just takes your noticing the child behaving well and commenting on it. You don't need special stickers or treats to positively reinforce good behavior. And truly, sincere praise from you will be more valuable to the child than anything tangible you could give him.

To be effective, praise needs to:

- Follow the good behavior immediately. If you say two hours later, "I liked the way you played with Molly in the block corner," it won't work as effectively.
- Be specific. If Johnny, who has a history of running in the house, walks calmly from the doll corner to the table for lunch, your saying, "I like the way you walked to the table, Johnny" is far more effective than simply saying, "Good job, Johnny."
- Be sincere. Kids can tell if you're being overly lavish with your praise or if you don't really mean it. For example, a calm statement like, "I saw the way you shared Duplos with Annie; that's great" is much better than, "Wow, you're the *best* cooperator in the whole place!"

Sometimes, when dealing with a particularly challenging child, it's difficult to praise the one thing she does well when eighty-five other things have gone wrong that day. You might be tempted to say, "Finally, you shared a toy!" rather than, "I like the way you shared the dinosaur with Andy." Keep in mind that any negative comparison will completely negate the praise. The following are a few classic misused praise statements:

Good. You picked up your toys. Try to remember to do it tomorrow.
That was a great throw for a girl.
That's a nice drawing. Why didn't you finish the top part?

Remember, when using praise, be specific, immediate, and sincere. The rewards, shown in children's self-esteem and behavior, will follow.

Attention

One parent educator I know is fond of saying, "You don't get to choose whether or not you give children your attention. You only get to choose how." It's true. If children don't get your attention by behaving well, they'll get it by behaving badly. If an appropriate bid for attention goes unnoticed or unattended to, it will most likely turn into a bid for attention that cannot go unattended to. Brenda gives an example of how children may choose to get negative attention rather than no attention.

> It was a rainy day and the children couldn't go outside to play as we usually do. Two of them asked me for a story instead. I was busy getting the afternoon's art activity ready and told them to find something else to do. The next thing I knew they were beating up on the dog. Upon reflection, I wish now that I'd read the story, or told them when I'd be available to read. It would have been a lot easier than calming the children and the dog down.

It's important to realize that attention can be positive or negative, verbal (praise or scolding), physical (a hug or a spanking), or nonverbal (listening or smiling). What kind of attention children prefer depends on their temperament, the type of attention they are accustomed to getting, and their skill level in asking for attention. Lisa talks about how the children in her care like to receive attention:

> At four and a half years old, Danielle is very active. She likes me to watch her climbing on the jungle gym and performing various tricks. Her favorite way to ask for attention is, "Lisa! Watch me!" She doesn't seem to want me to say anything, just to watch. Now her younger brother, Zach, age twenty months, likes physical attention. He wants me to hold him on my lap and read or just rock. Often he'll signal this need by clinging to my leg. Both of them, however, are quick to get my

attention by fighting with each other if I'm initially unavailable on the attention-front.

Teach children acceptable ways to ask for your attention. Some simple ways are:

- Saying, "I need a hug."
- Asking for help.
- Saying, "I need some attention."

You can decide what will work best for you and your mix of children.

Rewards

A reward is used to reinforce good behavior. It is given just following the behavior you want to see and immediately reinforces it. The reward has to be something the child really wants, or this technique won't be an effective reinforcer. Here are two examples of providers who've successfully used rewards.

> I watch each day to see who settles down cooperatively at naptime. The child who does this quickly and well gets rewarded by being the one to "wake up" the other children by tapping them gently with my magic wand. I whisper to this child before he goes to sleep. I rotate this reward so no one child gets it all the time, and sometimes no one gets it and I do the wake-up duty.

> My children have a hard time paying attention to directions. Listening carefully is something we're working on. When I observe a child really paying attention, I remark on it right away and reward him by naming him "lunch helper" for the day. The lunch helper gets to help me serve lunch.

The most powerful reward for a toddler is an adult's time and attention. Preschoolers like to get special privileges (like those described above), stickers, treats, or other kinds of special tokens. Try to rotate the rewards. If you use the same one all the time, then you give that item or privilege an exaggerated importance. It is also true that after a while, children become satiated with a reward and it begins to lose its attraction.

Be careful not to confuse rewards with bribes. A reward *follows good behavior* and reinforces it. A bribe is given beforehand or afterward to *avoid misbehavior*. While bribes will usually work if you use them on the same situation all the time, they only provide a short-term solution. It is far more effective to reinforce the behavior you want to see.

Andrea describes the following common example of a bribe.

> I had one mom who would tell her daughter, Anna, age two and a half, that if she didn't cry when she was dropped off at child care, she could have candy when she got home. It didn't work. Anna would cry anyway and half the time, the mom would still give her candy. Finally, I talked with the mom about developing a goodbye ritual to help Anna with the transition. She still cried for about three weeks, but after that, she settled down into the routine of child care.

If the mother in the example above wanted to switch to a reward system, she could have asked Andrea to give Anna a sticker each time she went through the goodbye ritual with her mom calmly.

As opposed to bribes, the techniques of attention, rewards, and praise have the added advantage of emphasizing the behavior you want. Children are much more likely to behave the way you want when they know *what* it is you want. Many children can tell you what behavior will get them into trouble, but they are far less clear on what adults want them to do.

Decreasing Difficult Behavior

When you put even just two children together, there's no shortage of difficult behavior. Providers—and parents—cite daily struggles with:

- Sharing
- Hitting
- Refusal to cooperate with normal requests
- Following rules (for example, No running inside)

- Eating
- Napping

As we've said before, reinforcing good behavior is the most effective way to get children to continue it, but when you've got a child who just can't seem to function in one area, then it's time to pull out a few tools to help him along.

This section will look at three techniques: ignoring, time-out, and setting consequences. We will also look at two techniques that are particularly effective with toddlers: changing the space and redirection.

Ignoring

This is an appropriate technique to use when a behavior is simply annoying (like crying to get attention) rather than a safety problem (like hitting). The idea is that you completely, absolutely ignore the offending behavior and it will die out from the lack of attention from you.

Brenda describes a successful case of ignoring:

Tenisha, age three, went through a phase where she would screech at the top of her lungs to get attention. This didn't seem to bother the other children, but it drove my assistant and me nuts. We decided that the reason she did it was to get our attention in order to solve her problem (usually boredom), so we decided to ignore it. The next time it happened we were out on the deck, watching the children play. Tenisha got bored with her truck and tried to take another child's toy. He refused. Tenisha screeched as loudly as she could. My assistant and I continued to talk normally over the noise. We didn't make eye contact with her or even look at her. She turned her head to see why we weren't responding. We felt a little silly, but started an intense discussion about the gate three feet ahead of us. We talked about that gate like it was the most important thing in the world. Tenisha screamed louder. And louder. After three minutes of this, she gave up and went to join two other children playing with a train. We had about two more incidents like this and then she stopped screeching altogether.

Ignoring only works if it is used every time the behavior occurs and absolutely no attention is paid to the child (even a glance). Don't try to distract the child by offering her a toy or treat.

Lisa shares her ignoring technique:

> When I ignore an annoying behavior, I go to a nearby toy corner and interest myself busily in playing. I might build an amazing block tower, or talk to a doll. I don't pay any attention at all to the child while he is whining, crying, or whatever. But when he stops and gets interested in what I'm doing, I will gently involve him in it and leave him to play on his own.

You may find certain behaviors so annoying that you can't help but give in and pay attention in order to stop them. If this is the case, don't use ignoring to decrease the behavior; try another technique.

Time-Out

This is a technique whose purpose is to remove a child from a conflict situation in order to give her a chance to calm down and try again. It is *not* a punishment.

Time-outs work best starting when a child is between two-and-a-half and three-and-a-half. The child needs to understand the concepts of "waiting" and "quiet." With toddlers, the time-out should last one minute or less. Use the one-minute-for-each-year-of-age rule for preschoolers. Here's a step-by-step description of how time-out is intended to work:

1. Misbehaving child is removed from conflict, rule is repeated ("No hitting") and adult announces it's time for a time-out.
2. Child is brought to a quiet, calm spot (like a couch or hallway) not too far away from the action and told to sit quietly.
3. Child sits quietly for the duration of the time-out (the timing begins *after* she has stopped crying, whining, or talking). Adult does not talk to, comfort, or discipline the child during this time.
4. At the end of the time-out the adult thanks the child for sit-

ting quietly, explains what kind of behavior is appropriate ("Touch gently") and invites the child to rejoin the play.

5. Adult watches and compliments child when she plays appropriately.

You will need to walk the child through this process one or two times before she understands how it works. After that, you should be able to tell her to take a time-out and have her go to the time-out spot. Remember not to start timing until all fussing has stopped.

This is a useful technique in child care because it allows the child a chance to calm down and then gives another opportunity to practice appropriate behavior. Do not abuse or lengthen the time-out period; several one-minute or less time-outs are more effective than one long time-out. The more chances a child has to practice appropriate behavior, the faster she will learn. Andrea describes how time-out works in her child care.

> All the kids in my care are very experienced with time-out. Some of them even seem to welcome the chance to take a break from the group and quiet down. Just yesterday Christopher was acting up during circle time. I told him to take a time-out. When I signalled him to return, he told me politely, "I'm ready to control myself now." And he was!

Be consistent with time-out and use it appropriately. It is fairly common for caregivers or parents to misuse time-out by allowing themselves to argue, being swayed by tears and promises to do better, or just responding angrily to rudeness. Here's an example:

> It seems as if you're half as effective with your own kids than with the child care kids sometimes. I can do time-out letter-perfect with the little kids, but when it comes to my own six-year-old, I blow it every time. He just knows how to push my buttons. When I send him for time-out he goes, but he makes obnoxious comments on the way about my mothering and by the time he gets there, I'm yelling enough to need time-out myself.

If you can't disengage from the conflict long enough to facilitate a time-out, the child won't be able to either. If you find yourself doing this, try another technique that works better for that child.

Setting Consequences

There are two kinds of consequences you can use with young children to decrease difficult behavior: natural and logical. Consequences are different from punishments; they are directly related to the child's behavior and always offer the child an opportunity to take responsibility for the misbehavior. Setting consequences works like this:

- *Natural consequences* happen automatically. If it's raining and a child doesn't put on her shoes when she goes outside, her feet will get wet and cold. If a child doesn't eat his dinner, he will get hungry before breakfast. These consequences are natural and don't need you to make them happen; they happen as a result of the child's action. They are valuable learning tools for young children who are just learning about cause and effect.

  Make use of natural consequences by pointing out what they will be. Chris describes how she does this.

  It was a bright, hot day and we were going to the beach. All the four-year-olds have child-sized sunglasses to wear. I instructed each of them to put his or her sunglasses in the beach bag before we went. Tanya refused to cooperate; she was busy with a block tower. I told her, "If you don't bring your sunglasses, you'll get bright sun in your eyes." She ignored me, so we went without them. Sure enough, the bright sun bothered her and she was jealous of the other kid's sunglasses. She complained to me about it. I sympathized about the bright sun, but reminded her that she chose not to bring her sunglasses. She was unhappy, but since then she has never failed to take her sunglasses to the beach.

  Natural consequences allow children to take responsibility for their actions and learn from them. Chris was wise not to solve the problem for her (buy her another pair, let her borrow another child's pair, etc.) but let her experience the natural consequences of her own decision.

Of course, allowing children to experience natural consequences is not appropriate in safety situations, such as stepping out in front of a car. Be on the lookout for opportunities where children can safely experience natural consequences.

- *Logical consequences* are created and administered by you. They should be related to the misbehavior, acceptable to you, and carried out immediately. For instance, "No splashing kids' faces in the wading pool. If you splash again, you'll have to get out." The consequence is related to the misbehavior and is one the provider is willing and able to carry out immediately.

The following is not an effective logical consequence: "No splashing kids' faces. If you do it again, you won't get a story later." The consequence here is not related to the offense and feels more like a punishment than a consequence.

Changing the Space

Altering the physical environment works well with young children, particularly toddlers. This is something that most providers do naturally. You lock up the knives, put the stereo equipment in rooms they don't go into, or keep the dog outside. But changing the space is also a useful tool for solving specific behavior problems. Here's an example.

> I had trouble with children climbing over and bouncing on the couch. No amount of reminders helped them stop—it was just too much fun. After some thought, I decided to make the couch much less convenient to get to. I rearranged the room so that the couch was off in a corner near the books and blocked by other interesting, active toys. It wasn't so easy to run across the room and bounce onto the couch—they had to walk around inviting items to get to it. Gradually, the couch became used for story time and the active play was confined to the middle of the room and outdoors.

You can cut down on chaos and problems by restricting certain activities to specific areas. For example, we only eat in the kitchen, make art at the table, play with sand outside, and so on. In this way you limit the environment.

You can also manipulate the children's space so that they can function more independently. A child-sized stool and low towel rack in the bathroom will free you up from constantly assisting with handwashing. Easy, low-level access to toys is also necessary.

Redirecting Children

Oftentimes a child does something unacceptable for the sheer joy of it. For example, toddlers enjoy ripping paper. Ripping up books, however, is unacceptable. In these kinds of cases, providing the child with an acceptable alternative is very effective. The toddler may not rip up a book, but he could rip up old newspapers. One provider gives an example of redirecting.

> Tyler, age three, loves to whack things. Inside or outside, he tends to find a bat, a stick, whatever, and whacks away. I worked very hard with him to help him learn that whacking inside is unacceptable. Outside, he can whack weeds or tree roots. Once we found an okay place for him to whack, the inside problems went away.

Toddlers will often easily accept this kind of substitution, but they will also test to see if you really mean it on Mondays, or when a parent is present, or if you're gone and your partner is in charge. This is normal. Be aware of such testing and firmly remind the child of what the rule is.

There are many, many ways to redirect children's play and exploration in acceptable ways. Train yourself to help children find better ways to explore.

Fostering Good Social Skills

All providers and parents want children to play together cooperatively, or at least without bloodshed. Some children have good instincts for getting along with others and other children need more teaching and guidance.

Concepts like sharing, negotiation, and problem solving are appropriate to start teaching at about age three. Before that, children do not have the cognitive skills necessary to deal safely with conflict without your intervention. The beginnings of teaching problem solving can be found in the technique "A Better Way" (described earlier). Children who are familiar with this tool will learn problem solving more easily.

You can do joint problem solving with a young child and you can help children begin to learn to solve their own problems. Elizabeth Crary, in her book *Kids Can Cooperate* (Parenting Press), describes the following problem solving approach, which she calls "SIGEP."

1. Stop. Calm yourself and the child(ren) down.
2. Identify the problem and feelings. State what the problem is in a factual, nonjudgmental way. Then state the feelings involved, using I-messages.
3. Generate ideas. Both adult and child(ren) think of all the ideas they can to solve the problem. The adult writes all the ideas down, even the silly or unworkable ones. Do not evaluate the ideas while you're thinking them up.
4. Evaluate the ideas. Talk about why each one might work or might not. Cross out the ideas that won't work.
5. Plan. Together, pick one of the ideas you both like and plan how you will implement it. If it doesn't work, go back to your list and pick another idea.

Debbie talks about how she used this approach with a child who had a very hard time separating from her mom in the morning.

> Corrie, age three and a half, cried every morning after her mom left. Most of my kids will quickly get interested in playing after their parents leave, but Corrie was sadder than most, I think. She would cry for half an hour sometimes. I decided to try some joint problem solving with her. I rocked her for a few minutes and then said, "You feel really sad when your

mom has to go to work." Corrie nodded and kept crying. "Hmmm," I said, "how could we solve this problem? Let's think of ways for it to be easier for you to say goodbye to your mom." Corrie just continued to cry.

"You could keep a special picture of your mom in your pocket," I suggested. The crying quieted a bit as Corrie got interested in what I was saying. "Or," I went on, "we could ask your mom to call you at snack time in the morning."

"We could stay home," Corrie insisted.

"That's one idea," I responded, "what's another idea?"

"She could play a game with me before she leaves," Corrie offered.

"Or," I said, "you could ask me for a hug if you feel sad. That's a lot of ideas. I don't think your mom can stay home from work all the time, so that won't work. Which of the other ideas do you want to try?"

Corrie decided she wanted her mom to play a game with her before she left and to call at snack time. I spoke with the mother that evening and she agreed to arrive ten minutes earlier for a game and to check in on Corrie by phone.

Joint problem solving is especially effective because it offers the child some control and "say-so" in how the problem is solved. If a child has helped choose a solution, then she has much more invested in seeing it work than if it was handed down from above.

Research shows that when faced with a conflict, the more alternatives a child (or adult) can come up with, the more likely he is to choose a solution that works well. There are three easy ways to model the problem-solving process for children.

First, you can model the process by using it to work out your own conflicts. For instance, one provider consistently uses problem solving with her own, older children in front of the children in care. It's also helpful to "think out loud" about problems in order to model solving them. For example, "Let's see. Maria wants me to help her wash her hands and Josh needs me to watch him on the monkey bars. That's two children who need me at the same time. I can't be two places at once, so what can I do? I could make Maria wait for help, make Joshua wait for me to watch, ask Lily (the teenage helper) to help Maria, or I could help Maria and watch Josh from the bathroom window. I think I'll try that. Is it okay with you if I watch from the bathroom, Josh, or would you like to wait?"

Second, you can model the process with puppets, dolls, or stuffed animals. Pick any problem you commonly see the children having, like sharing a toy, and have the puppets act out the problem. Talk about their feelings. Then ask the children for ideas on how the puppets might solve the problem. Listen to all the ideas, being careful not to discount any (if a child suggests something inappropriate, like, "Smash him in the face," then redirect the energy by saying, "Hitting and smashing are hurting ideas. What are some helping ideas?"). Then have the children choose one idea. Have the puppets act out the solution. If it doesn't work, point that out and have them choose another idea. Remember to keep talking about each of the puppet's feelings as they try different solutions.

Third, you can use children's books to illustrate problem solving. There are many excellent books that specifically use this process and others that are easily adaptable to it. Elizabeth Crary's series on problem solving is especially useful; it covers the common conflict areas of sharing, waiting a turn, entering a play group, name calling, getting lost, and separating from a parent. Sarah, an experienced provider, shares this story about using Crary's book *I'm Lost* with her group:

> My kids weren't used to these kinds of problem-solving books at first. At the beginning of the story, the main character gets separated from her dad at the zoo. "What can Amy do?" I read. One little girl eagerly raised her hand and suggested, "She could give up and go live with the gorillas!" It was hard to keep a straight face, but I said, "Well, that's one idea. What else could she do?" We continued on and the children quickly caught on to the real-life nature of the story.

Traditional stories can also be used to model problem solving. One provider liked to use the classic story *Curious George* by H. A. Rey to do this.

George gets into a lot of mischief. I'd point out the problem as he got into it and ask, "How does George solve the problem?" The children (who have read this book seventy million times) would tell me exactly what will happen. "What else could he have done?" I would ask. After a while, they got into thinking up new ways for George to escape whatever trouble he was in.

Appendix lists several books that are helpful in fostering good social skills in children.

Where to Go When a Child Needs More Help Than You Can Give

All children have behavior problems from time to time. Some children, however, exhibit behavioral disturbances that require help past what you can provide. Typically these children are asked to leave several child care settings due to chronic acting-out behavior. (Most parents of these children will not inform you of the child's history.) The difficult behavior might include hitting, screaming, constant refusal to cooperate, biting, spitting, foul language, and so on. Also of concern is a child who is extremely introverted or fearful. There is usually a physiological or psychological reason for a child's continued difficult behavior—and since you are neither physician nor therapist, it is better to refer the family to someone trained to help.

Although it is much more common for children to be excused from family child care due to problems with the parents, you may occasionally ask a child to leave for behavioral reasons. In general, it is wise to refer parents to your local Resource and Referral agency. The agency can direct them to other professional help or a therapeutic day care, if appropriate. It is also wise for you to call the agency and advise them that you've dismissed the child and for what reasons; this protects you as well as helps the agency properly refer the family.

7

Back to Business

This chapter attempts to give you a broad overview of record keeping and taxes. Since tax laws are continually changing, it is inevitable that some information will change during the print life of this book; readers should always check their understanding of tax rules with the IRS and/or other qualified professionals. The information conveyed here is not intended in any way to take the place of legal, accounting, or other professional services.

Three areas that are important to your business will be discussed: 1) generating enrollment, 2) setting up your office, and 3) record keeping. A successful business depends on all of these to some extent.

Generating Enrollment

You can't run a family child care without the children, so one of your first orders of business should be to generate enrollment. The sooner you operate at your capacity, the sooner you will be profitable. There are several ways to go about marketing your child care service.

- *Sign up with your local child care Resource & Referral Agency* as soon as you are licensed. They refer their callers to all appropriate child care options in the area. You were probably put in touch with your local Resource & Referral when you went through the licensing process. If not, locate the nearest agency by phoning the National Association of Child Care Resource & Referral Agencies (see the Appendix).
- *Hand out or post printed materials advertising your child care.* Have some business cards made. Most communities have printing shops that offer a business card service. Black ink on a white card is usually the least expensive and can look very professional. If you have an artist friend, have her sketch you a logo in black ink to have reduced and put on the card. Keep in mind that you cannot reproduce just any drawing you find; most are protected by copyright. However, you can buy books of "clip-art," drawings that are published with the express permission that they may be duplicated. Ask for this kind of book at your local bookstore or library.

The following is an example of a provider's business card.

BAKEMAN FAMILY CHILD CARE
Serving parents of children ages one to five years

Barbara Bakeman, proprietor
8080 Trellis Drive, Bellevue, WA 98005
206–555–4234

Another printed piece you can create is a flyer that advertises your service. This flyer can be posted in dozens of locations in your community (with permission), including the local grocery store, church or synagogue, children's clothing or bookstores, restaurants, beauty salons, laundromats, personnel offices of large employers in your area, and so on.

Here is an example of one provider's flyer.

SUNSHINE FAMILY CHILD CARE

A full service family child care providing loving care
for children ages birth–six years.

- Fully licensed home child care.
- Preschool curriculum program for ages three to five.
- Flexible hours: 6:00 A.M.–5:30 P.M., Monday through Friday.
- Participant in Federal Food Program.
- Discounts for second child in care.
- Convenient location.
- Reasonable rates.
- Owned & operated by former preschool teacher.

Located at:
54322 Redondo Beach Drive
Santa Theresa, CA 92533
Proprietor: Mary Nichols

PHONE: 808–925–7765

CALL NOW

When preparing your flyer, try to focus on the *benefits* a
parent will receive by coming to you—such as discounts for
more than one child—rather than listing features (such as
your big backyard). Start by looking at how other providers
have put together flyers. Your local or regional child care association can help you collect some of these.

Make sure you include, in large letters, directions for what
an interested parent should do. For example, in the above
flyer, the Sunshine Family Child Care tells parents to "CALL
NOW!" and gives the phone number in big numerals.

You can have flyers typeset and printed at your local printing shop. If you (or a friend) has a nice desktop system, you can typeset the flyer yourself. When getting ready to print the flyer, take time to look over the selection of papers and inks. Ask to see samples of how certain color combinations work together. If you've seen a flyer you especially like, take it in as a sample and ask the printer for an estimate on printing your flyer with the same or similar paper and ink. Always, always get an estimate before you place a print order. Keep in mind, too, that every change you make as you progress will cost you extra money.

• *Name your business with marketing in mind.* Think about the area where you are located and the families you will service. The two child cares represented above have very different types of names. "Bakeman Family Child Care" is straightforward and would appeal, say, to those, in a university community. If you are competing with several child care centers in the neighborhood, something like "Sunshine Family Child Care" is more eye-catching.

Here are some other examples of business names:

    Andrews Family Child Care
    The Strawberry Patch
    Kiddie Corner Day Care
    Rainbow Kids Child Care
    The Happy Kids Place

Your choice of a name depends on how you want your business to be perceived. I recommend choosing a name that communicates child care and warmth, but sounds like a business. Brainstorm a few possible names and then run them by your neighbors, friends, and associates before you make a decision.

Something else to keep in mind is that in the event of an audit, the IRS typically responds better to businesses that operate in a businesslike fashion, and have a name that sounds like a business. If you are operating without a business name, you will appear more as a babysitter to the IRS than as a businessperson.

• *Put your business name on your checks.* Even if your bank account is in your name, you can add "dba" (doing business as) and the child care name—for example, "Susan Townsand, dba The Secret Garden Child Care."

Deborah, a long-time provider, talks about this method of marketing.

I've always put my child care name on my checks. You'd be surprised how many clerks and merchants notice it, comment on it, and ask me about my business. Half the time they are looking for child care or know someone who is.

In order to use a dba or business name (anything other than your own name), you need to file a fictitious business name statement with your city or county. Go to the bank where you'd like to open up your business checking account. They can advise you on how to proceed. In some communities, the local newspaper handles the application for you; in other areas, you need to go directly to a government office. You will be asked to fill out a form describing your business (answering, for example, is your business conducted by an individual? partners? is it a corporation?) and to present identification. There will be a filing fee. In addition, you must take out space in your local paper that informs the public of your fictitious business name. Find out when your statement expires (generally it's five years); you will need to refile at that time.

As you go about this process, check to make sure that no one else is using the same business name. Your local library can help you with this kind of name search.

- *Talk up your business: Word-of-mouth is, perhaps, the very best way to fill your child care.* Tell everyone you know that you are opening a child care or have spaces to fill. Inform your relatives, friends, former colleagues, neighbors—anyone you come into contact with. Word will spread.

One provider describes how this works for her:

When I first started doing child care, I began by caring for a few friends' children. I expanded with referrals from my R & R and from my church and soon was filled up to my capacity. Now I get calls at least twice a month. I prefer to take referrals from my group of parents; I trust their recommendations more than any other referrals I get.

- *Network with other family child care providers in your area.* Keep a list handy of their numbers and agree to refer any callers to them if you are full; in turn, they will refer to you when they are full. You can get in touch with other providers through your local child care Resource & Referral agency and your local family child care association.
- *Classified or display advertising* is also an option. Providers' opinions vary on how effective this really is. In general, it is better to advertise in the small, local weekly papers in your community than in the large dailies. An even better option is your community's parenting newspaper or magazine (for example, *Baltimore's Child, LA Parent,* or *Northwest Baby*).

When placing a classified ad (the most cost-effective) remember that every word costs you money, so be concise. Here is a sample classified ad:

> **Family Child Care:** openings for kids 1–5 yrs. Licensed, experienced provider. 7 am–6 pm M–F. Valle Vista area. Call 927-8222.

If you are placing a small display ad, scan the publication for other ads the same size that catch your attention. Make sure the service you offer (family child care), the area you are located in, and your phone number are prominent.

- *Have sweat shirts or T shirts printed for yourself,* your assistant, and the children with your business name and logo on it. Wear them when you go out on field trips, or even to the grocery store. People will notice and comment on them. An added bonus is that matching shirts helps you keep track of the children while you're out. (*Note:* Do not put children's individual names on the shirts—it makes them vulnerable to abduction.)
- *Keep your child care clean and tidy* when parents come to visit, drop off or pick up their children; it will help you keep them enrolled. A messy or dirty child care will not reassure parents or encourage them to place their child with you.

Camille talks about her system for keeping things tidy when parents walk in.

I make clean-up part of the daily schedule. I vacuum early in the morning before anyone arrives. The children help my assistant and me to pick up before circle time (about 1:30 P.M.). Then at 5:00 P.M. we have mandatory video watching in the study while my assistant quickly picks up the main play room and vacuums. The parents arrive at 5:30 P.M. I really feel the clean play area helps sell parents on family child care.

The above strategy works well for Camille. Some parents, however, may object to mandatory videos—however educational they may be. Be sensitive to parents' priorities in this area.

Not all of the marketing ideas described here will work for you, but some of them will. Undoubtedly, you will have ideas of your own. Faye, a provider of about one year, shares the methods that worked for her:

I wish now that I'd started advertising the business the minute I started the licensing process. It's taken me about nine months to fill up to capacity. The things that worked the best were 1) Big posters posted on utility poles (made with thick black felt markers on neon-orange colored poster board), 2) Referrals from our R & R, and 3) an ad in The Eastside Parent newspaper. We also ran an ad in the local daily paper, but that didn't get even one call.

Many providers also report that spring is a good time to generate enrollment. There are a few reasons for this: Some providers close for the summer, many schools are ending their school year, and families often move in the late spring and summer.

Screening Parents and Children

Experienced providers often recommend some kind of screening process once you've attracted potential customers. If possible, you want to avoid "problem" parents and children (for example, parents who have left a previous child care with unpaid bills, are chronic offenders of the late pick-up policy, who neglect their children, and so forth, or children who have behavioral problems beyond your ability to cope with).

You can screen prospective clients by inviting the parent and child in one evening (after child care hours) for a brief meeting and tour of the child care. You'll want to get some important information from the parents. Here are some possible questions or points to cover in your meeting:

- Where was the child last in care? (Get a name and city and then later call the provider for a reference.)
- Why did you leave? (Press the parent to be as specific as possible. For example, if a parent replies vaguely, "It didn't meet our needs" then probe further; "What specifically didn't you like?" or maybe, "From what you said earlier, it sounds like there might have been a personality conflict. Was that it?")
- To detect potential problems with late pick ups, go over your hours of operation in detail, emphasize that you have little, if any, flexibility and then ask, "Will this work for your schedule?"
- Does your child have any special needs?
- Discuss your guidance policy with parents and then ask, "Will this be consistent with how you handle discipline at home?" If you have radically different guidance philosophies, then that should surface here.

These are only a few of the most common screening questions. You will undoubtedly have more to ask as you observe the parent and child. Some providers routinely ask for one or two former child care references in writing. If appropriate, suggest the child and parent spend an hour or two one morning with you and the other children; this way you can observe how the child interacts with others.

If you are considering two or more children for one space, let the parents know; if you decide against one family, it is a more graceful way to decline enrollment.

Lastly, remember to advise parents of your probationary period for all children (see chapter 3). If you and the family are a bad match, there's an automatic way out for both of you.

Setting Up Your Office

Many new providers are so enthusiastic about setting up the space for the children, they neglect to set up office space for themselves. You won't need a lot of space or equipment, but having a space specifically designated for your after-hours business work will help you stay organized and on top of the paperwork.

A desk in the study, kitchen, or bedroom can easily do the trick. One provider uses her formal dining room as a business and planning space. This area needs to be clearly off-limits to the children and possibly off-limits to your family as well.

Answering Machine

It is almost essential for you to have an answering machine for your telephone. When you are caring for the children, they are your first priority—not the telemarketer, neighbor, or relative on the line. Deborah, an experienced provider, describes her use of an answering machine.

> I couldn't get along without it. My message goes something like this: "Hi, this is the Strawberry Patch. All hands are on deck right now, but if you'll leave your name and number, I'll get right back to you." I tell all the parents that if they call during the day, they will most likely get the machine. I check the calls very regularly and return them as promptly as possible. I haven't had any complaints from the parents.

Not only do answering machines allow you to focus on the children, they help with your marketing: Prospective parents who call don't have to hear the noisiness of the children—you can return the call during a quiet time of day, and you can be sure you won't miss the call. An added bonus is that a polite message on the machine reminds your friends and family that you are at work and not available for visiting on the phone.

Filing System

You will be keeping track of many pieces of paper in the course of running your business. You will need to keep attendance records on each child as well as medical consent forms, immunization records, meal records, and so forth. When the state inspector comes to visit, she will want to look at your files on the children. If the IRS pays a call, they will also want to see that you've kept your receipts and information for tax deductions in a systematic, orderly manner. The moral of this story is: You need easy access to this information in some kind of file cabinet.

Many of us have a home filing system already. If not, you can buy small file cabinets new or used or purchase cardboard or plastic file storage boxes. It is easiest to set your filing system up at the outset, rather than creating it as you go. To start out, prepare file folders for the following:

Children's Files

1. Attendance records (including dates when care began and ended).
2. Parent-Provider Agreement (Signed!) This agreement should include child's full name, address, age, birth date, parents' home and work phone numbers and addresses, and any special needs the child has.
3. Medical Consent form (See samples on pages 35 and 36–37), which should include an adult emergency contact if both parents are unavailable.
4. Signature list of those authorized to pick up child.
5. If you do not carry liability insurance, you need a signed

Business Files

1. Record of income by week (can be combined with child's attendance records).
2. Meal records (for CACFP)
   A. Number of children who ate breakfast/snack/lunch/dinner each day.
   B. Record of money reimbursed to you by the food program.
   C. Copies of your menus.
3. Record of miscellaneous income.
4. Records of expenses by quarter
   A. Direct expenses
   B. Indirect expenses
   C. Capital expenditures
   D. Start-up expenses
   E. Food receipts for child care
   F. Family food receipts

statement from the parent acknowledging this.

6. Copies of any correspondence or notes you've taken on the child's care.

7. Copies of any W-10 forms given to parents for the year (see p. 184).

5. Quarterly tax file (for copies of finished forms).

6. Tax record archive (this will more than likely be a box you store in an out-of-the-way place).

7. Records of your business hours.

8. Bank statements, receipts, and returned checks.

9. File for licenses or permits that are not required to be posted.

Some of these categories we've gone over in detail already; others—the expense and tax categories—we will cover in depth later in this chapter.

Computer and Printer

Expensive hardware and elegant software are not "must-have" items. You can run your child care efficiently with an old-fashioned typewriter and a nearby copy shop. But if you have a home computer, you can make good use of it. Most providers with access to computers use them for word processing or accounting purposes, such as:

- Typing up a handbook of child care policies for parents.
- Creating templates for parent-provider agreements.
- Creating flyers or notices of special events, schedule/rate changes, etc., for parents.
- Using home-office invoicing software to bill parents.
- Using home-office accounting programs to keep track of expenses and deductions.
- Creating banners and other graphics for the children to enjoy.

Providers vary in what kinds of programs they like to use. Most use the word-processing program they learned before they started doing child care. *Microsoft Word* and *Word Perfect* are two popular word-processing programs. When it comes to the nitty-gritty of home businesses, many providers like to use Intuit's *Quicken* (which includes a check-writing program for paying expenses) or, from the same publisher, *Quick Book* (which differs in that it offers an invoicing feature). *Cash Pro* by Striata is another checkbook program for small businesses.

You do not need to invest in complicated software systems designed specifically for child care programs if you are first starting out. However, as you establish your child care and decide to stay in the business, it is smart to look to the future. And you may decide that a software system for child care programs would be beneficial to your business. If you do, keep the following points in mind as you shop for software.

- *Will it meet your needs?* Know ahead of time what you want the software to do: billing, keeping attendance records, daily schedules, and so forth. Don't be distracted by peripheral features. To be considered, the program needs to meet your primary needs.
- *Will it be easy for you to learn and use?* You won't have a lot of time to sit in front of the computer terminal and worry each step through. All programs advertise themselves as easy to use, but we all have different learning styles and speeds. The best way to answer this question is to try the system out; get a demo disk or find another provider or center who uses the program and ask for an overview.
- *Does the program provide customer service support?* In other words, when you get stuck, is there someone at the company you can call? All reputable programs provide customer support, and if you're lucky, a toll-free number to access it. You'll need support the most when you install and start using the program.
- *Is the program guaranteed?* Make sure you get a written warranty that protects you if the software is defective or turns out to be completely wrong for your child care.
- *Can you really afford the program?* Many programs are costly and some will require you to buy hardware you do

not already own. When shopping, get the full estimate of what the system will cost you and weigh it against your income and expense projections for the year.

The appendix provides a list of general business software as well as software specifically designed for child cares.

Record Keeping

Well-known family child care tax specialist Tom Copeland says, "Taking care of children is only half of your job. The other half is taking care of business." This section will look at the most important business records you will need to keep.

There are two umbrella categories to pay scrupulous attention to: *records of income* and *records of expenses*. Family child care providers are not exempt from paying taxes. You will need complete, accurate records of what money you bring in (income) and how you spend it (expenses) in order to file a tax return.

How much time you spend on keeping income and expense records accurate and up-to-date (as you incur them) will dramatically affect your profitability as well as your mental health come April 15 each year.

Some Good Advice

Tax consultants who work with family child care providers are unanimous in their recommendation to keep business and personal records as separate as possible. Providers (and other home-based businesses) need to be particularly careful about this. The IRS views any crossover of personal and business expenses with suspicion. There are many ways you can safely separate your family expenses and income from those of your business. Here are a few tips for starting out:

- Open a separate checking account for your business. Deposit all business income in this account. Pay as many business expenses from this account as you possibly can.

  For those occasions when the expense is shared by your

business and your family (like food), pay for it out of your family account, and then reimburse your family account with a check from your business account (properly documented).

When you pay yourself, write a check from your business account to your family account. Document it as a transfer of funds.

Keep all your bank statements and cancelled checks for both accounts.

- Many providers have a credit card that is exclusively dedicated to business expenses. This is a good idea. Some companies, like American Express, provide you with monthly reports of expenditures. Keep all your statements and reports.

The government requires you to save all your records and receipts for three years. If you buy something and do not get a receipt (or lose it) make a receipt for your own records, as shown in this example.

Date:	10-1-94
Name:	South Prairie Used Book Sale
Address:	442 Main St., South Prairie, WA
Purchase:	five books at $1.00 each
Paid:	$5.00 cash

Income

The majority of your income will come in as payments from parents. For each payment received, you need to record:

- Child's name
- Amount paid (along with check number or receipt number if paid in cash)
- Dates of care covered by the payment
- Date payment was received

Most providers use a simple payment record. An example of a monthly record appears on page 183.

Monthly Record

Child	Sept. 1–5	Sept. 8–12	Sept. 15–19	Sept. 22–26
Sarah Anderson	$85/ck 458 pd 9-1-94	$85/ck 466 pd 9-8-94	$85/ck 467 pd 9-15-94	$85/ck 472 pd 9-22-94
Jonathan Carr	$45/ck 222 pd 9-1-94	$45/ck 238 pd 9-8-94	$45/ck 245 pd 9-15-94	$45/ck 253 pd 9-22-94
Eric Gray	$85/rcpt 45 pd 9-1-94	$85/ck 876 pd 9-8-94	$85/rcpt 49 pd 9-15-94	$85/ck 912 pd 9-22-94

The provider in this example cared for three children during September. She collected $85 a week for the full-time children, Sarah and Eric, and $45 a week for one part-time child, Jonathan. For the most part, the parents paid with checks; however Eric's mother paid in cash the weeks of September 1–5 and 15–19 and the provider noted the number of the receipt given her. We can see that our provider collects payment each Monday for the week she's providing care.

More sophisticated calendars are available for keeping combination records of your income and the children's daily attendance. Specifically, I recommend *Calendar-Keeper: A Childcare Record Keeping System* published by Redleaf Press; this calendar allows you to keep very specific track of each child's attendance, payment records, and meal plan participation all in one place. Combining some of these records, once you understand what is required of each, can save you time. One provider's combined time sheet and billing form for charging by the hour (which she chooses to do since she cares for many part-time children) is shown on the facing page.

The second source of income you will receive is money from the Child and Adult Care Food Program. Although it functions like a reimbursement (you get so much money, per child, per meal paid to you), the IRS currently views it as income and it is therefore taxable. The records you will be required to keep in order to participate in the food program will be very useful to you come tax time. Most providers report this income on their Schedule C as "Gross Receipts or Sales." If, however, your food program sponsor gives you a Form 1099, then you must also indicate on your Schedule C that you are declaring this "reimbursement" as income.

Other forms of income you may receive are bonuses or gifts from parents, or grant money from local or governmental organizations for buying equipment or other business items. Some providers care for low-income children and are paid by the state instead of the parents. Income from any of these sources needs to be recorded and described as well.

At the end of the year, many of your parents will ask you to fill out IRS Form W-10: *Dependent Care Provider's Identification and Certification*. This form asks for your social security number or tax identification number. Many parents are eligible for a tax credit on their child care expenses and will report how much they've paid you for the year. The W-10 does not ask you

Sample Attendance/Billing Sheet

Name: _____ Billing Month: _June_ 1994

Date	Time In	Initials	Time Out	Initials	Total Time
16 Wed					
17 Thurs					
18					
19					
20					
21 Mon					
22 Tues					
23 Wed					
24 Thurs					
25					
26					
27					
28 Mon					
29 Tues					
30 Wed					
31 Thurs					

Billing Calculation:

_____ hours (days)   x $_____ per hour (day) = $ _____

_____ absent/short days x $_____   min. per day   = $ _____

Previous balance $ _____

(+) _____

New Balance Total $ _____

to report how much each parent has paid you; however, it is in your best interests to have your income figures match the parent's expense figures for child care. (The IRS will be tempted to investigate if parents report spending more than you report earning). Many providers routinely give (or mail) each parent a report and receipt of their total child care expense for the year and have it signed. This helps ensure that everyone's figures are accurate. Another good idea is to routinely give parents a W-10 at the end of the year, whether they request it or not.

Some providers fear that parents will not be honest and will inaccurately report how much money they pay you in order to gain a higher tax credit. If this is a concern, explain to the parent that if your figures do not match, there is a strong likelihood that both you and the parent will be audited.

Expenses

There are three kinds of expenses: *direct business expenses, indirect business expenses,* and *capital expenditures.* You will have all three and you may deduct all three on your taxes. You will want to claim as many deductions as you are legally entitled to because this will reduce your taxable income that much more. There are, however, specific rules for what you may and may not deduct, and the IRS is continually changing its guidelines. This section will give you a broad overview, but does not attempt to cover every question you might have—for that you'll have to consult an accountant. Additional resources for figuring your expenses and taxes are listed in the Appendix.

Before you do your first set of taxes, you will need to calculate your Time/Space Percentage. This figure tells you what percentage of your home is used for business. The IRS considers it a reliable figure for determining what percentage of your home expenses are deductible as business expenses.

Time/Space Percentage

This is a figure that helps you calculate how much of any expense shared by your business and your family (with the exception of food) can be deducted on your business taxes. For example, if your Time/Space Percentage is 25 percent, then you may deduct 25 percent of your mortgage interest, rent, utilities, and other household expenses. We will look specifically at what you can deduct using the Time/Space Percentage later in this chapter.

To figure out your Time/Space Percentage, you need the following information:

- *The number of hours your home is used for business in one year.* You can do this by adding up the total number of hours you spend caring for the children, planning activities, cleaning for the business, keeping records or doing paperwork for the business, working on generating enrollment, and so forth. In short, any time you spend *in your home* working on business.

  Since you are just starting out, it will be easy for you to keep a daily log of time spent on business. A sample day's time record might look like this:

Tuesday, 11-15-93		
7:00–7:30 A.M.	Cleaning	.5
7:30 A.M.–5:00 P.M.	Caring for children	9.5
5:00–5:30 P.M.	Cleaning	.5
7:00–7:30 P.M.	Activity planning	.5
7:30–8:00 P.M.	CACFP paperwork	.5
	Total hours	11.5

Keep these kinds of records for every day you work in your home. Should you ever be audited, you will have highly accurate records of your time to back up your figures.

I recommend separating out the categories (child care, cleaning, planning and preparation, etc.) and adding up your total hours every month (just as in the above example) for two reasons: 1) At tax time you will simply need to add up the total twelve months worth of time to figure your time percentage; in the event of an audit, you can show that you really did spend this much time on business and exactly what it entailed; 2) You can scan these figures each month to make sure that the time you are putting into your business in each area is reasonable for the amount of money you are making.

Now, take the total number of hours worked in your home for the entire year, and divide it by the total number of hours in a year. For instance, let's say you worked in your home 2,765 hours for the year. Your time percentage would look like this:

$$\frac{2{,}765 \text{ (hrs worked)}}{8{,}760 \text{ (hrs in a year)}} = 31\% \text{ Time percentage}$$

- *Number of square feet in your home used for child care.* Count every room in your house that is regularly used by your business. Most providers use their family room/playroom, living room; kitchen, bathroom, laundry room, storage rooms, some bedrooms, and space such as entryways, hallways, and attached porches or decks. You may count your garage if you use it for storage of child care items. You may not include your lawn, swimming pool, patio, or driveway. See IRS Publication 587: *Business Use of Your Home* for more information.

   "Regular use" is usually interpreted as use during the majority of time your business is open throughout the year, not necessarily every day. So, if you use your spare bedroom three of the five days you are open, then that constitutes regular use. If you only use it once or twice a week, you might not be able to count that space. (*Note:* Check with your tax consultant each year for changing definitions and rules.) When you are faced with decisions in gray areas, always think about how you would justify the decision to the IRS in the event of an audit; thinking this way can help you make a good decision.

   You may already know the square footage of each room in your home. Or you might be like the rest of us and need to measure the rooms. Do this by getting out your tape measure, then multiply the length (in feet) of the room by the width; this will give you the area in square feet. Add the size of all the child care spaces together. Then divide that figure by the total square feet in your home. For example:

$$\frac{1,450 \text{ (square feet used for child care)}}{2,000 \text{ (square feet in home)}} = 72.5\% \text{ Space percentage}$$

The provider in our sample has a time percentage of 31 percent and a space percentage of 72.5 percent. To get her Time/Space Percentage she needs to multiply these two figures:

$$31\% \times 72.5\% = 22.5\% \text{ Time/Space Percentage}$$

The provider may deduct 22.5 percent of her household expenses from her taxes.

You will need to recalculate your Time/Space Percentage every year. Report it on *Form 8829: Expenses for Business Use of Your Home* with your taxes.

Direct Business Expenses

The IRS defines a direct business expense as an "ordinary and necessary" cost of running your business. Tax form Schedule C for businesses lists the following categories as direct business expenses:

- Advertising. This includes most of your marketing: ads, flyers, posters, buttons, and so on. (Business cards fall under office expenses.)
- Bad debts. Unfortunately, you cannot claim an unpaid bill by a parent as a bad debt. But if a parent does not pay you, be sure not to report this unpaid money as income.
- Car and truck expenses. You can deduct car expenses in two different ways. Most providers prefer to use the standard mileage rate method. At the time of this writing, the standard rate was 28 cents per mile. This figure covers all costs associated with using a car for business: gas, repairs, maintenance, and insurance.

To use this method, you keep track of your starting and ending odometer reading, the total miles travelled that trip, the date, and the destination. Get a daily organizer/calendar (such as a *Daytimer* or *Franklin Organizer*) to keep track of mileage and other business records. Two sample entries in your log could look like this:

11-3-94. 11,090 to 11,095. 5 miles. Safeway Grocery Store.
12-5-94. 11,150 to 11,165. 15 miles. Field trip/Discovery Zone.

At the end of the year, you add up your total miles for the twelve months, multiply that figure by .28 (or the current rate) and you have your deduction for car expenses for the year.

The other method for figuring car expenses is to calculate the actual car costs incurred by your business. This is more time-intensive, but may yield you a higher deduction. You must calculate the number of miles you drove your car for your business and divide that figure by the total number of miles you drove your car in the year; then multiply that figure by 100. For example, if you drove your car for 1,000 business miles, and 10,000 miles total for the year then your business use is 10 percent.

$$(1,000 \div 10,000 = .10 \times 100 = 10 \text{ percent})$$

You may then deduct 10 percent of all your car expenses.

- Employee benefit programs. It is unlikely you will be starting off hiring employees and giving them benefits (health insurance, profit-sharing programs, etc.), but if you do, you may deduct these costs.
- Insurance. Smart providers carry liability insurance for their businesses, whether they are required to by the state or not. You may deduct 100 percent of this expense. (Renters and homeowners insurance is covered under indirect expenses.) Car insurance is not deductible unless you use the actual car costs method of figuring your deduction (as described above).

Rules regarding health insurance change often; consult your tax accountant before claiming this. Disability and life insurance are not deductible.

- Interest. You may deduct 100 percent of interest charged on items you've purchased for exclusive business use. Use your time/space percentage to calculate deductions on items purchased for joint business and personal use.

- Legal and professional services. A tax preparer or consultant you hire provides a professional service. Other services included here are legal fees and services and accounting/bookkeeping services. Report these expenses on Schedule A.

- Office expenses. A host of expenses comes under this category. Some of the more common office expenses are bank service fees; office supplies such as paper, pencils, envelopes, and so on; postage; resources for your business use such as software, books, and magazines; supplies for record keeping such as calendars, forms, receipts, and ledgers; training and classes (except those connected with licensing); photocopying costs; and membership dues in professional organizations such as the National Association of Family Child Care or the National Association for the Education of the Young Child.

  If in doubt about the eligibility of an office expense, consult your accountant or tax adviser.

- Rent of business property. This covers the rental of items for business use, such as a carpet cleaner, not your monthly house or apartment rent.

- Repairs and maintenance of personal property. "Repairs" refers to repair of items damaged by your business. For instance, if one of your children in care hides M&Ms in your VCR, the repair bill is fully deductible. If your own child did it, then you may use your Time/Space Percentage to deduct the business percentage of the bill.

  Maintenance refers to all cleaning and maintenance supplies for your home that are necessary to run your business. A list of all the cleaning supplies you probably need would take up the rest of the book, but the top five might be cleansers and detergents, soap (dishwashing and hand), paper towels, toilet paper, and mops and brooms. Highlight these supplies on your grocery and drug store receipts to separate them from food.

Cleaning and maintenance costs are usually deducted using the Time/Space Percentage, since these are costs generally shared by home and business.

- Supplies. This is a big one. You will be purchasing many supplies for children's activities and care over the year. If they are used exclusively for business, you may deduct 100 percent of the cost (for example, children's books). If you purchase an item that you use after hours for the home (for example, a booster seat) then you need to use your Time/Space Percentage to figure your deduction.

  "Supplies" is an umbrella category that covers the following types of expenses: children's activities and toys, items for children's care (cribs, bibs, potty seats, and so on), and kitchen supplies (dishes, utensils, garbage bags, and small appliances).

  Keep records of all these purchases and how you determined the deduction.

- Taxes and licenses. Fees you incur during the licensing process (permits, fire inspections, license fees, and so forth) are 100 percent deductible. If you hire an assistant and pay payroll taxes, then those are also deductible.

- Travel, meals, and entertainment. When you travel to a conference or training session, you may deduct the full cost of your transportation by car (using the standard mileage rate), plane, bus, or train, as well as lodging. You may deduct 80 percent of your food and entertainment costs only if they are associated with business.

- Telephone. Sorry, the IRS will not allow you to deduct the monthly cost of your first phone line into your house. If you have a second, separate business line, it is 100 percent deductible. You may deduct long-distance business calls, services like call-waiting, and phone repairs, using your Time/Space Percentage.

- Wages. This covers the wages you pay to employees (your assistants). Do not include in this category independent contractors (for example, the clown you hired for the birthday party, or the graphic artist who designed your business cards). Do not include the money you pay yourself. (Note: The graphic artist's fee is a legitimate business expense and would be included in the advertising category. The clown may or may not be deductible—check with your accountant.)

You must report wages on Schedule C, while payments totalling $600 or more per year to independent contractors are reported on Form 1099-Misc: *Miscellaneous Income*. If you are confused about whether you have an employee or an independent contractor on your hands, consult your accountant right away; there are serious penalties for failing to file correct forms and pay taxes on employees.

- Other: food, household items, yard supplies. Food is one of your major expenses. It is also, for the vast majority of providers, a shared expense between business and home. Muster up all your precision and nit-picky abilities to keep your food receipts as accurate and detailed as possible. When conducting an audit of a family child care provider, the IRS will zero in on your food records right off the bat. They do this for two reasons: 1) They can't quite believe your family isn't gobbling up all the food you've purchased and the children are brown-bagging it; and 2) Many providers are lax about keeping their grocery receipts, and thus cannot document their food expenses.

Here are a few tips for doing it right.
  - Try, as much as possible, not to purchase food for both your family and the child care in the same trip to the grocery store. If you must, separate the food and have the clerk ring up two purchases. Pay for the child care food out of your business checking account.
  - Save every single food receipt. Believe it or not, IRS Publication 587: *Business Use of Your Home* asks you to keep *all* your personal food receipts as well as all your business ones. This means your personal grocery store receipts and any restaurant receipts. Although it sounds like a lot of work, saving your personal receipts actually protects you in the event of an audit; you can easily show what you spent to feed your family as opposed to what your

business food expenses were. The former is usually much higher. Save the food receipts in weekly batches.

In addition to your receipts, Tom Copeland, a well-known tax consultant for family child care, recommends you also save the following records:

1. Check stubs or cancelled checks (spent on food).
2. Copies of your child care menus.
3. Attendance records (to show children were present and ate the food).

- On your receipts, mark each item to show if it is a business, personal, or shared expense. (Remember not to include supply items, like aluminum foil and toilet paper, in the food category. Mark them for your supply expenses.)
- After you have been collecting and marking receipts for a few months, try to estimate your weekly food expenses. Do this using your receipts and menus for five or so randomly selected weeks. Remember not to include food you and your family eat. When you come up with a figure, you can use this at the end of the year to give your food receipts a "reasonableness check." If your weekly food cost estimate is $75, you were open for 45 weeks that year, and your yearly receipts total $3375, you're right on the money. If your yearly receipts are significantly higher or lower, then you know you've got an error somewhere.

You may not use your Time/Space Percentage to figure your business share of food costs; therefore, it is very important for you to keep accurate, ongoing records.

Household items include things like safety barriers, tools, fire extinguishers, bed linens, and so forth. Yard supplies would be items such as garden hoses, sandboxes, and lawn mowers.

You should report all the above-described direct business expenses on Schedule C.

Indirect Business Expenses

Also called "house expenses," indirect business expenses are specific costs you have in maintaining your home. Typically, you use your Time/Space Percentage to figure the deduction you may claim. Note, however, that you may not show a loss in your business for the year from claiming these expenses. These expenses should be listed on IRS Form 8829. The specific costs are described below.

- Mortgage loan interest and real estate taxes. If your Time/ Space Percentage is 25 percent, then you may deduct 25 percent of your mortgage loan interest and real estate taxes for your business on Schedule C. The remaining 75 percent can be deducted on your personal taxes, Schedule A.
- Casualty losses. A casualty loss is damage to or loss of property from events like earthquakes, floods, accidents, or vandalism. This is what you have home or car insurance to cover. However, if you do not have insurance, or the insurance has a deductible, your out-of-pocket cost from the damage or loss is an indirect business expense. Use your Time/Space Percentage to figure what percentage of the cost you may deduct.
- Insurance on your house. You may deduct a portion of house insurance or renter's insurance as an indirect business expense.
- Utilities. Use your Time/Space Percentage to deduct the business portion of the money you spend on electricity, oil, gas, water, sewage, and garbage.
- House repairs and maintenance. All homes need yearly upkeep. Items in this category could include painting (inside and out), fixing broken windows, servicing the furnace, and so forth. Be careful not to include any repair or maintenance of personal property here, just what is pertinent to the useful life of your house. Major home improvements (adding on a room, enclosing a porch) are not covered in this category (see "Capital Expenditures," below). Check each year for any cost limits on this category.
- House rent. If you rent your home, you may deduct your Time/Space Percentage for the rent.

Capital Expenditures

A capital expenditure is the purchase of any one item for your business that will last more than one year. For example, the following are often claimed by providers as capital expenditures:

house, couch, computer, refrigerator, car, or adding on a new room.

The IRS is concerned mostly with items costing $100 or more. Capital expenditures wear out gradually, year after year. Because you don't "use them up" all in one year, you may only deduct a year's worth of use. This practice is called depreciation. It is complex and the government likes to change the rules frequently. Once you start depreciating a purchase under a certain rule, then you continue with that rule for the purchase until the item wears out.

Since you are just beginning your business, consult an accountant or tax preparer on current depreciation rules and practices. You will be able to depreciate portions of the following:

- Your house.
- Major home improvements. (This differs from a home repair in that the improvement increases—not just maintains—the value of your home.)
- Land improvements. (These are permanent improvements that increase the value of your property, such as landscaping, fences, or tennis courts.)
- Personal property. (For example, computers, furniture, TVs, major appliances, and so on.)
- Start-up expenses. (After you have begun the licensing process but before you are ready to accept your first child, the purchases you make are considered start-up expenses and are subject to depreciation or amortization—the cost spread evenly over five years. Most purchases under $100 you make after you have started caring for children are considered direct business expenses.)
- Automobile. (You can depreciate the cost of your car if you are using the actual-expenses method instead of the standard mileage method of claiming expenses.)

If the item wears out or its use is discontinued before the end of the depreciation period, you may deduct the remaining amount to be depreciated in the year it wore out.

Reporting and Filing Your Taxes

We've covered income and expenses in the sections above, including routine references to the federal tax forms you will need to report these. The following is a brief list of forms and publications issued by the IRS for you to gather as you get ready to file taxes.

Schedule C: *Profit or Loss from Business*
Schedule SE: *Self-Employment Tax*
Form 1040 ES: *Estimated Tax for Individuals*
Form 1040: *US Individual Income Tax Return*
Form 4562: *Depreciation and Amortization*
Form 8829: *Expenses for Business Use of Your Home*
Form W-10: *Dependent Care Provider's Identification and Certification*
Publication 334: *Tax Guide for Small Businesses*
Publication 583: *Taxpayers Starting a Business*
Publication 505: *Tax Withholding and Estimated Tax*
Publication 587: *Business Use of Your Home*
Publication 917: *Business Use of a Car*

(If you hire employees [assistants]):
Form W-2: *Wage and Tax Statement*
Form W-4: *Employee's Withholding Allowance Certificate*
Form W-3: *Transmittal of Income and Tax Statements*
Form SS-4: *Application for Employer Identification Number*
Form 940: *Employer's Annual Federal Unemployment Tax Return*
Form 941: *Employer's Quarterly Federal Tax Return*
Form 1099: *Miscellaneous Income*
Form I-9: *Employment Eligibility Verification*
Circular E: *Employer's Tax Guide*

(Of possible use to you as you continue in your business)
Form 1040 X: *Amended US Individual Tax Return*
Form 5305: *Simplified Employee Pension*
Publication 590: *Individual Retirement Arrangements*

Form 1040 and Schedules C and SE are the backbone of your taxes. The other forms deal with documenting and supporting your income and deduction claims and those taxes associated with having employees.

Lots of providers show a loss in the first year or two of business. This is generally due to a combination of start-up costs and a slow build-up of enrollment. Such a loss is considered normal. The IRS becomes concerned when you don't show a profit for three out of every five years. If you do show consistent losses, you are more likely to be audited; the IRS may decide that you are not serious about making money and merely have a hobby, not a business, and then disallow your business deductions.

There are several sections in this book dealing specifically with business concerns that will help you become profitable; consider carefully how they apply to you and your business. Family child care can be a successful and profitable career for you, but it demands that you function in a businesslike manner.

A Final Word about Taxes

Don't be daunted by the complexity of figuring and filing taxes. No one can know everything about tax law. As long as you keep accurate, orderly records, follow IRS instructions, and get help when you need it, chances are you will be just fine.

I recommend you attend workshops on record keeping and taxes for family child care providers. Find out about workshops offered in your area from your local family child care support group, your local R&R, or your food program sponsor. I highly recommend Tom Copeland's books about this subject, *Family Child Care Tax Workbook* (updated every year), and *Basic Guide to Family Child Care Record Keeping*.

When you're looking for a tax preparer, try to find one who is thoroughly familiar with family child care. Ask your colleagues who they use, or ask your R&R for a referral. Not all accountants and tax preparers are educated about the unique tax situation your small business is in.

8

Solving Common Problems

Every business comes with its problems, and family child care is no exception. This chapter will look at some common problems providers have in dealing with parents, with their own family, with the age-mix of the children in care, and with friends and neighbors.

Problems with Parents

Most providers rank parents as their top problem. As one provider put it, "It only takes two out of fifteen parents to make your life miserable." Problems commonly develop over communication, attitudes, guidance philosophy, late pick-ups, and non-payment.

Communication and Attitudes

The best way to avoid communication problems is to have written policies that parents sign when you agree to care for their children. When conflicts over things like payments, pick-ups, or sick children come up, you can state your position and refer them to the parent-provider agreement.

Faye describes some parent communication problems she's had:

> I had one set of parents who were not very honest. They made a lot of excuses for not abiding by the terms of our agreement. One of my policies is that parents will call me in the morning if a child will be late or absent. Somehow their daughter was late a lot without my being notified. These parents also would drop their daughter off in the morning and expect me to take her to a doctor's appointment if they couldn't make it. We had talk after talk about these problems, but to no avail. I finally had to terminate care.

Remember too, a parent-provider agreement is a two-way street. You must enforce your rules and policies or you will teach the parents to disregard them. For example, if it is your policy that children going through potty-training not wear overalls and you find one child turns up every Thursday in his Osh Kosh B'gosh specials, then you need to speak to the parent about it. If you don't, the parent learns that your policies can be ignored without repercussions. Other parents, who love to dress their children in those cute little overalls, will notice your permissiveness and resent it, or begin to follow suit. You do no one a favor if you allow parents to abuse your policies. If you find that a particular policy is no longer relevant, then put the policy change in writing and distribute it to the parents.

Possibly most wearing on providers are parents who have "attitude problems" or, as one provider put it, "are just plain obnoxious." Camille describes the complaints she has fielded:

> It always tends to be the same parents who gripe. They complain about another child having a cold, or about spilled paint on clothing, or that little Joshua said he was starving when he left child care the night before—it just goes on and on. I make it a routine to greet each child and parent at the door in the morning and then see them off at night. If little Joshua fell outside and scratched his elbow, then I tell the parent about it

and how it happened. Likewise, if he comes in the next morning with a bump on his forehead, I ask how he got it. I don't want the parent coming in later and thinking that he got it here. And, my state requires that I document such things.

Besides complaints, which are usually straightforward, some providers report more subtle attitude problems. Faye, a provider and also the parent of adult children, runs a family child care with her partner and daughter-in-law, Tina, who is the parent of a two-year-old. The partnership works well for them in terms of their differing expertise and in sharing the workload. Some parents, however, show an inappropriate tendency toward age-discrimination—they dismiss Tina as "not the adult in charge." Faye describes the situation:

> The way we have things organized, Tina arrives at my house at 6:00 A.M. to set up and cook breakfast. She greets the early-arriving children and parents. I don't come on duty until about 7:00 A.M. Some parents insist on speaking to me about a concern, even though we've repeatedly told them that we're partners and they can consult with Tina about anything.

Faye and Tina have dealt with this sort of subtle disrespect on an ongoing basis. They made a conscious decision to have Tina initiate discussions with parents on their children's needs, child care policies, and other routine matters. They report that slowly but steadily parents are showing more respect for Tina's role.

Some providers report that being older than the parents, and in many cases having raised their own children, places them in a more confident position. "Parents perceive you as having more authority," says Camille, "and you feel less intimidated by the parents when you've been through the child-raising years yourself."

Camille goes on to warn against giving advice routinely or encouraging parents to lean on you. Parents who are unusually stressed, emotionally needy, or just plain immature can drain you with requests for information and support. "Know your limits," she advises, "and don't get overly involved with any one family."

All providers report that if you think providing quality child care will cause parents to express appreciation, you're in for a resounding disappointment. One state inspector puts it this way, "Parents are not out to find wonderful child care, pat you on the back, and reward you handsomely. They're cheap and out to find a bargain." A five-year provider adds this, "Never, never do family child care as a favor to the parents; they will not appreciate you as they should. Charge enough money to feel amply compensated." Another provider agrees, "You have to learn to reward yourself; parents won't do it for you."

Most providers agree that the rewards in family child care are many, but they come in the form of the work you do with the children, the money you make, and the support you get from your colleagues—not in appreciation from parents.

Differing Guidance Philosophies

Ideally, your initial interview process and your written policies should help you sniff out any parents with dramatically different philosophies from yours. But sometimes they slip by you. Lisa describes a situation where this became a problem.

> I cared for a special-needs child, Krista, age four, who has hydrocephalus and is in a wheelchair. I thought my guidance philosophy was clearly spelled out in my policy, but this child's parent decided that my policy didn't apply to a child with such health challenges. She lets Krista bite. Biting is not acceptable in my child care, so I brought it up with the mother. Her position was that the other children, who were not physically challenged like Krista, should be tolerant of her behavior. I was unwilling to change my policy on this for anyone, so needless to say, we soon parted ways.

Again, clear policies and quick communication when there is a problem will help you prevent and deal with situations like these.

Late Pick-ups and Nonpayment

No provider is immune to late pick-ups (from every once in a while to chronic offenders) and an occasional parent who doesn't pay her bill, or who pays late. It's annoying, a headache to deal with, and it will happen to you.

Chapter 3 goes over suggested policies for handling these particular problems. The important thing to remember is to *do what your policy says you will do.* If you state that you will charge $5.00 for every minute a parent is late, then you must keep track of when the parent comes in and charge him/her, no matter how reasonable the excuse. If a parent bounces two checks and your policy states that she then must pay up-front, in cash, then you must require that. If she fails to do so, then you need to terminate care.

Don't be afraid to exercise the termination clause in your parent-provider agreement. If a parent consistently abuses your policies or fails to pay you, then you have just cause to ask the parent and child to leave. It is not fair to you, your business, and your family to allow parents to abuse your time and services. If a parent leaves angry or with an unpleasant attitude, notify your local child care Resource and Referral agency; tell them exactly what happened and why you dismissed the child. Keep written records of what happened (for example, document the nonpayment on the specific dates, keep copies of written notices to the parent, and make notes of any discussions you have with the parent). Then if the parent goes to the R&R with a complaint or accusation, you will have documented the events leading to your action.

Problems with Your Family

Chances are, even if you have involved your family in the planning of the business and brainstormed on ways to cope with the sacrifices all family members will have to make, you'll encounter a few bumps on the way. No matter how prepared you and your family are, there will be problems from time to time. This is normal. Experienced providers offer solid advice for coping with these times.

Complaints from Your Spouse

Most providers report their spouses to be wonderfully supportive of the business. These providers are also careful to structure
the business day so that overlap with family life is minimal.
Spouses' main complaints are about sharing space and your time
with the business.

> My husband's beef about the child care was having kids
> around after my 6:00 P.M. "closing." I made my late pick-up
> policy much more strenuous and enforced it more regularly.
> The late pick-ups subsided dramatically and my husband re-
> laxed more.

Keeping work and family as separate as possible will prevent
problems. Providers who expect their partners and children to constantly give up family time and space to the business after-hours
soon deal with serious problems. Try to strike a balance between
their needs and yours. One provider describes her experience.

> We haven't had too many problems. At first, Bob resented the
> planning and paperwork time I needed in the evenings to or-
> ganize the business. We worked out a deal where I confined
> my after-hours work to Tuesday and Thursday evenings from
> 7:00–9:00 P.M. while he looked after our kids' needs. Then
> after 9:00 P.M. I was available to him and the kids.

Problems with Young Children

Your own children are understandably not very happy to share
you. Some adapt well and like the activity and interaction of the
child care. Others have a hard time adjusting to the invasion.
Providers agree that the number one problem children ages two
to five have is sharing their mom. Here are two accounts from
providers.

> Jason was four years old when I started my business. At first,
> he intensely disliked my paying attention to the other kids.
> Since the business was my way of being able to spend more
> time with Jason, we persevered. We talked about ways he

could ask for my attention without resorting to tantrums and we also looked at the best times of the day he could have my time. I set up a star chart for him to reward him for the times he asked for attention appropriately. When he got ten stars I took him to McDonalds for lunch. After a while, things calmed down. He started to like the other kids better, although he was usually ready for them to leave by 3:00 P.M. instead of 5:00 P.M.

My five-year-old daughter had trouble sharing me. We worked out a special time just for her. When the kids in care were napping, she was allowed to choose a special game for me to play with her.

Like the provider above, you may find it effective to establish a special time that your young child has exclusively with you, every day. It doesn't have to be during business hours, but it does have to be consistent and belong entirely to the child. Don't use the time to teach your child and don't choose the activity yourself. Let him decide what you will do together (even if you have to play *Candyland* for thirty days in a row) and follow his lead. If you consistently offer your child quality, focused time with you, his behavior at other times will generally improve.

Difficulty in sharing mom is followed closely by being asked to share toys. In general, children aren't developmentally capable of sharing until ages three to four. Forcing two-year-olds to routinely share their toys will buy you much misery and little peace. Providers vary in how they deal with this.

I make my own kids' toys off-limits to the day care. My kids are not allowed to bring them out into the playroom unless they are willing to share them with everyone (it rarely happens). Consequently, all the day-care toys must be shared—no exceptions. This has worked pretty well for us. For some reason, my kids are not territorial about their books; they're quite willing to share them, so that's not an issue.

My budget is not very big, so when I started the business, I planned to use my three-year-old daughter's "big toys" (kitchen center, ride-on toys) in the daycare. We talked about which toys she was willing to share with the other kids. I didn't force her to share any toy she didn't want to—and she surprised me with how generous she was. All her nonsharing toys had to stay in her room. I also allowed her to change her mind about sharing a toy, but she had to make the decision at the end of the day when the kids were gone, not in the midst of play.

Issues of sharing parents and toys are very common with this age group. Be sensitive to your child's needs and honor her preferences whenever possible.

Problems with School-age Children

Your school-age child, ages six to eleven, is usually better about not demanding your constant attention, but sharing issues continue to crop up. School-age children are typically much more territorial about their rooms and toys, as described in the following accounts.

> My son is seven. We worked through his concerns for privacy and privilege by making his room private and off-limits to the business and by allowing him to choose his own snacks (but he always had to eat them away from the other kids).
>
> Jenny is eight. She likes the children in care, especially the younger ones, but is bothered by the older ones being in her room or playing with her things. I need to use her room for naptime, so we worked out a deal. I pay her "rent" for the time the other kids are in her room. All toys are off-limits and put away unless she decides she wants to rent a certain toy to the business. This way she has a concrete benefit when she's required to share.

School-age children also like having some attention when they arrive home from school. Adjusting your schedule—perhaps the other children can have free play at that time—will allow you to focus on your own child for a brief time.

There are many ways to deal with your children's concerns. Networking with other providers and discussing options will give you more ideas.

Problems with Older Children and Teens

Older children tend to ignore the child care in favor of their own agenda. Many providers report these kids are just "hardly ever around." Some of the same issues do appear, however.

One provider had trouble with her middle school–age kids wanting to boss the little kids around. They felt their space invaded and attempted to maintain some ownership by controlling the children. The mom in this case solved the problem by encouraging her older kids to invite friends over (or visit other friends' houses) and socialize with them while the child care was open. This way their focus was on their friends—not on the children being cared for.

Another provider shares her story:

> I have three teenage sons. They like the kids and will occasionally help out. Their biggest complaint, though, is "You give all the good food to the day-care kids!" We addressed this problem by involving them in the family shopping so they could have some control over what food was available. I also worked out a system where, if nothing else appealed, they could take child care food (I keep it separately) and write down what they ate.

The provider above not only had to record what food was eaten by her teens, she then had to subtract the cost from her business expenses.

Coping with your own children's needs will take some creativity and flexibility on your part, but it is worth it. A happy, supportive family is something a family child-care provider needs in order for her business to be successful.

Problems with a Multi-age Mix of Children

We all know that life with young children can be easier if they have someone around their own age to play with. They play together better and their needs are similar. Life is not perfect, however, and you will undoubtedly not end up with conveniently matched pairs of children in care.

The Benefits

There are some definite benefits to having a multi-age mix of kids. First, you can accommodate siblings. It is important to many parents that their children be together in child care. This is a special feature that a family child care is equipped to provide. Child care centers almost always separate children by age; *you* can have them all together in a homelike atmosphere.

Second, it is a good learning experience for children to be around other age groups. They can learn appropriate ways to play with younger children, and they can learn from the older children. It is a great self-esteem booster for children to be able to help and look out for each other and family child care is an ideal place to foster this behavior.

The Challenges

A multi-age mix does bring with it certain problems. Experienced providers recommend that you carefully plan the age-mix you accept for care. Accepting six children of different ages is asking for trouble. One provider recommends seeking children who are the same age as your child as a place to start. Another prefers to take children from ages two up to five (pre-kindergarten), although she'll take a child as young as twelve months if he or she is a sibling. She explains her age limit:

> I find the kindergarteners are usually too big for many of the toys I have. They're also a bit more disruptive. I guess they feel they've outgrown the child care setting.

Making rules based on ages is often effective for avoiding chaos. Lisa describes how she handles a mix of two- to five-yearolds.

> I don't let the younger two's do circle time with the others— they're just not ready for it yet. Another thing I do is put out

toys and puzzles on two ends of my long play table; the younger toys at one end and the older toys at the other. I also find it's helpful to adhere strictly to the "only four kids playing with the housekeeping toys at one time" rule.

Another provider adds that she makes it a rule the older children (ages five and six) not play with the smaller toys with intricate pieces around the children age two and younger. They can play with these special toys during the younger children's naptime.

Assistants Come in Handy

Most providers agree that a broad age-mix is most easily handled when you have an assistant or partner. Many advise against taking infants unless you do have an assistant, since babies take up so much more time.

Tina describes how she and her partner, Faye, handle their broad age-mix:

> Since there are two of us, I take the older kids downstairs for more structured preschool activities and Faye keeps the younger ones with her upstairs. During the summer time, we all go outside together where there's more space.

Deborah, a provider in a sunny climate, uses her outdoor play area on a daily basis.

> My assistant has story time inside with the younger kids while I take the older ones outside for free play. Then we trade places.

Providing care on your own without an assistant does not automatically mean that you will go crazy with more than two age groups present, but it does mean that you will need to be very, very organized. A common problem time is when you need to prepare food or clean up and still watch the children.

Laura describes how she handles the problem spots:

> I use my look-through window from the kitchen to the family room to keep an eye on the kids while I'm cooking or cleaning

up. The secret is to keep food preparation quick and simple. I serve snacks that are easy to prepare and quick to clean up. Another thing I commonly do is put on a favorite video (about twenty minutes long) for the kids to watch while I'm preparing lunch; that keeps them quiet, occupied, and all together.

Minimizing Interruptions

If you've ever been home with children or worked out of your home, you already know that friends, family, and neighbors tend to interrupt at the least opportune time. When you have six young children to watch, you can't have Aunt Bernice calling up to chat about the family reunion or your neighbor dropping in.

Deborah, a long-time provider, addresses the problem:

> You just have to educate people. When they call or stop by, tell them that you can't talk while the children are in care and give them an option or two when they can call back or drop by again. Most family and friends are understanding once you explain it to them. I also highly recommend getting an answering machine and using it. Train yourself not to pick up the phone if you are involved with the children.

Everyday problems in child care are inevitable. The good news is that some provider somewhere is sure to have experienced a problem like yours before. Belonging to your local and regional Family Child Care Association groups will put you in touch with other providers. Attend meetings and ask for help when you need it. Going to special seminars and other educational events will also help you solve these kinds of problems in ways that work for you.

9

Planning for the Future

Planning is a natural part of a new venture. However, at the outset many providers forget to plan for growth of their business. Even as you're starting out, you should think about if, or how, you want to expand. Business growth that simply mushrooms without careful planning will leave you overwhelmed and possibly ready to close up shop. Too much demand without a plan for meeting it has often been the undoing of many a small business. Healthy growth is a matter of making choices ahead of time and careful planning.

Small versus Large License

After two years or so, many providers with a small license are often ready to upgrade to a large license (seven to twelve children); others are happy staying where they are. Staying small and growing larger each presents benefits and trade-offs. Let's look at some of these.

Small License

Benefits

- No need to alter space for additional children
- Opportunity to raise fees regularly and improve certain features of the business
- No need to hire help and increase paperwork
- Less stress on own family

Trade-offs

- More of a cap on income— much reduced potential for income increase
- Less creative challenge as you become experienced with the business and its size; more potential for boredom
- Fewer "extras" for family due to smaller income

Large License

Benefits

- Increased income
- Opportunity to work with other adults (assistants)
- Increased creative challenge
- More flexibility with setting fees
- More flexibility to take part-time children
- More "extras" for family due to increased income

Trade-offs

- Increased work
- Obliged to hire assistant and assume all the responsibilities of an employer
- Obliged to meet state requirements for large license (possibly increase space)
- Higher probability of job burn-out
- More stress on own family

These are some major concerns to think about; you will undoubtedly consider many more ramifications on your own. Start giving growth some thought now. Later in the chapter we will look at specific goals for providers as you go along.

At this start-up point, there are several areas you need to think about when it comes to planning for the future.

Your Physical and Emotional Well-being

If you plan to care for young children day in and day out, then planning to be in good health and carrying out that plan is critical to the long-term success of your business. All providers agree it is paramount you take good care of yourself and find support when you need it. "After a week with young children," says one provider, "you can feel it."

Working and living with young children requires a high level of energy. Camille shares her thoughts on this:

> I would say that having lots of energy is even more important than liking children! (Especially if you are caring for babies.) I had to cut one of my assistants down from four to three days a week, just because physically, she was burned out by Thursday.

Faye agrees:

> The most important thing for me is getting lots of sleep. I used to work in child care some years ago and had to quit because I injured my back from lifting the kids too much. This time around I strictly limit the lifting—nothing too heavy. The changing table is set exactly for my height. I also make sure I get massages as often as possible—that helps me relax and stay in tune with my body.

Taking care of yourself means getting adequate sleep, eating right, and exercising regularly (by yourself, not with the children). In addition, find ways to nurture yourself, like having regular massages or manicures. Providers agree that you should *not* give up hobbies or activities that are special to you, like piano lessons, book groups, or playing on a softball team. Lisa talks about how she protects her leisure time:

> I have a fellowship group at church every Wednesday night. It's important to my mental well-being for me to go. I sent out a notice to all the parents letting them know that they must be on time to pick up their children on Wednesdays. I accomplished this by beefing up my late fee schedule and then enforcing it strenuously on Wednesdays.

Another important way to be good to yourself is to take vacations and holidays. Don't give in to the temptation to work on your time off or take in just one or two kids. You need the breaks.

If you do not take good care of yourself, you may become ill or burn out on family child care. It is hard to keep your capacity up if you are continually getting sick and requiring parents to find substitute care. The parents and children need to depend on you to stay healthy and provide consistent care. You can only do so by paying good attention to your own needs.

Planning for a Substitute

There will be occasions when you cannot be at work. Going to an educational conference, dealing with a family crisis, or having the flu are just a few examples. You will, of course, attempt to keep these occasions few and far between. Instead of cancelling child care for the day and forcing parents to fend for themselves, it is nice if you can provide a substitute.

One way to do this is to use your assistants (if you already have them), provided they are adults—you must always have at least one adult present with the children. Some providers have an arrangement with a friend, relative, or neighbor who is a stay-at-home mom; this friend agrees to substitute for your planned absences in your home for a daily fee. Additionally, she agrees to make herself reasonably available for your unplanned absences. This substitute is usually not required to be on your license, although if you use your spouse, as Deborah does in the example below, then it can be convenient to have his name on the license.

Deborah planned ahead for absences:

When I upgraded from a small license to a large one, I put my husband on the license. He's not a daily part of the business, but has agreed to substitute for me—as the responsible adult on the premises—when I need to be away for family child care meetings. His job is such that he is able to take a day off here and there without any problem. All the parents know him and it makes a fun change for the children once in a while.

Another option is a substitute service. These are similar to the substitute pools that schools use; they are not yet widespread, but they are growing. Your regional family child care association or your local child care Resource and Referral agency can tell you if there is such a service near you.

Whenever you bring in a substitute, you need to leave her or him fully equipped to keep the children safe, fed, and occupied on a schedule that is as close as possible to your own. Make sure your substitute has a copy of your daily schedule; is familiar with your emergency route out of the house; knows the location of the fire extinguisher and emergency phone numbers; has a copy of the menu for the day; and is briefed on any special needs the children have.

Hiring an Assistant

When your child care is established and you are reasonably profitable, you may consider hiring an assistant. If you are expanding your license, then in most states, you will be required to hire help. Having someone to help out and share the burden is usually well worth the extra expense and paperwork involved.

Julie, who has a large license, describes her assistants:

> I employ an adult woman in the mornings (I have two who job-share) and a teen helper in the afternoons. I had no trouble finding them. The women are stay-at-home moms who wanted to earn a little extra money; I found them via friends at church. I found my other helper by calling up my local high school home economics department and asking for possible candidates.

An assistant can help you with many things. Below is a list of some ways that having an assistant will make your job easier and more enjoyable.

- You are free to go to the bathroom, answer the phone, and feel confident that the children are safe.
- An assistant can supervise the children while you are preparing food or cleaning up.
- An assistant can monitor activities in progress and help sense when it's time to move on.
- An assistant can help prepare art activities and assist the children as they do projects.
- You have someone to share with; children are always doing something charming and priceless, or challenging and obnoxious. An assistant is someone to celebrate and commiserate with.
- It's good for the children to have another caregiver around. Often, you will have one child you just don't relate well to; many times your assistant will cope better with this child than you can.

This last point is illustrated by Laura, a provider of four years:

> I have one little girl, Amanda, age four, who is prone to screeching when she wants something. I've had demanding children before, but never one who gets on my nerves like she does. After some thought, I realized that she reminds me a lot of my oldest son at the same age—it was a hard time for both of us. I asked my teen helper, Malia, to make a special point of attending to Amanda. This gave me a nice break in the afternoon, which allowed me to relax and tolerate Amanda a little better. She responded well to the attention from Malia and her screeching diminished a bit.

Hiring employees also brings with it certain responsibilities and challenges. If you've ever worked as a manager or business-owner before, then you know firsthand all the snags that tend to crop up. By the time you hire an assistant, you probably will have settled on a style and daily routine that work well for you. Introducing a helper to your child care day will change your pattern. Whether those changes will be for the good or bad depends on how well you make your expectations known and how open you are to new ideas.

Camille, who has had assistants for the past two years, shares the problems she's encountered.

> I wish my assistants would take a little more initiative in planning the daily activities and in seeing that something needs to be done and doing it without waiting for me to tell them to. I also have to watch that we don't end up with "dead time" where the assistant sits and listens to me during circle time, or visits too much with the parents instead of working.

Job descriptions are helpful. They tell the assistant exactly what you expect of her and you can refer to the job description when you meet with your assistant to review her performance. A sample job description for a part-time assistant is given below.

When you are ready to hire an assistant, there are many places you can find good candidates. Like Julie in the example

---

JOB DESCRIPTION

Title: Child care assistant
Hours: 2:30–5:30 P.M., Monday through Friday
Salary: $6.00 per hour
Description: Responsibilities will include assisting provider with:
- Preparing, serving, and clearing meals
- Preparing materials for art and other activities
- Leading certain activities such as storytime and selected games
- Accompanying children on outings to the park or more special field trips
- General crowd control
- Clean up of playroom, kitchen, and bathroom
- Planning of activities
- Ensuring the safety and well-being of all children in care

earlier, you can find people through your own personal network of family, friends, church, or other groups you belong to. Mothers who are choosing to stay at home with children sometimes welcome the chance to earn a little extra money and still have their children with them (however, you need to have room in your capacity to accommodate these children). The early childhood or home economics departments in your local high schools, community colleges, and universities have job boards where you can list the position you have open. Your local Resource and Referral agency also offers a job bank for those interested in working with children.

The hours you offer depend on your needs and the state's requirements. If you have a large license, then you are most likely required to have an assistant present when the seventh child arrives. Many providers have a morning and afternoon assistant, with little, if any, overlap. Wages for this position are generally paid by the hour and vary according to where you live. To avoid over- or under-paying assistants, network with other providers in your area to find out what they offer as a starting wage. Your local Resource and Referral agency may also be of help here. Also check federal and state minimum wage laws (if your state minimum wage is higher than the federal—and it usually is—then you need to meet the minimum wage for the state).

Most providers choose to hire a single, part-time assistant or a combination of two or three part-time assistants. Hiring one or more part-time employees is generally simpler and less expensive for your business than hiring a full-time employee (which is different from a full partner). Full-time employees are entitled to certain benefits such as overtime wages and any benefits you provide for yourself (pension, vacation pay, health insurance, and so forth).

Lastly, do not overlook the fact that when you hire an employee, the IRS requires you to deduct and pay social security and federal income taxes (together, these are known as "payroll taxes"). In addition, you must pay federal (and sometimes state) unemployment taxes. See chapter 7 for the specific IRS forms you will need to file. Refer also to Tom Copeland's *Family Child Care Tax Workbook* (Redleaf Press) for a detailed and helpful disussion of how to correctly keep and file this tax information.

Increasing Your Fees

Another key ingredient to long-term success is planning your fee increases. There are many reasons for raising your fees. The most common are:

- Rising expenses
- Increased expertise or education on your part
- Accreditation of your child care (see page 222)
- Improvement of your facility or other improved features of the care you provide
- Upgrading to a large license and hiring an assistant

Right now, think about when you realistically might increase your fees. Set a date, perhaps six months from opening, to review your fee schedule and expenses and to calculate your profitability. If you are running in the red, you need either to reduce expenses or to increase fees immediately. If the situation is not critical, but you feel a fee increase is appropriate, set a reasonable date for doing so. Give parents at least one month's notice of the fee increase. More than one fee increase per year is viewed unfavorably by parents, so figure your calculations and make plans carefully.

Plan to review your profitability on a regular basis. If you make your fee increases at consistent intervals (for example, every year in June), parents will be more comfortable and less likely to leave you for other care.

Camille, a successful provider of about five years, increases her fees yearly.

I notify the parents of the fee increase in June and then put it into effect in September. I find yearly increases, even as small as fifty cents a day, are more effective than a larger increase once every three years. Parents accept the smaller, regular increases more readily.

Networking: The Importance of Being Well-connected

Plan to plug into your local, regional, and national family child care networks. One very important source of support will come from your colleagues in the form of professional associations. No one will understand your problems and successes like another provider.

As discussed in chapter 2, joining the National Association of Family Child Care (NAFCC) is a good place to start. They can put you in touch with your regional group, send you their newsletter, *The New National Perspective*, and offer you resources to order by mail. In addition, they sponsor both national and regional conferences.

Another pertinent organization is the National Association for the Education of the Young Child (NAEYC). Membership is open to those who work with young children in all types of settings—day cares, preschools, child care centers, universities, and so forth. Like NAFCC, NAEYC has many regional and local branches and sponsors conferences and workshops on all levels. In addition, they publish a bimonthly magazine, *Young Children*. Addresses for both NAFCC and NAEYC are located in the Appendix.

It is not always practical to attend national conferences, but whenever they fall near you, make every effort to take a couple of days off and attend. They are a wonderful opportunity to hear nationally-known speakers on early childhood topics, and a plethora of useful, practical workshops are there for the taking. In addition, these conferences almost always sponsor an exhibit hall of vendors who are eager to sell you books, toys, and teacher resources. If you live far away from any major city, chances are these national conferences won't be held near you, so look to your state and regional conferences. They are often just as helpful, though not as big.

Another organization worth knowing about, although you probably do not need to belong on the national level, is the National Association of Child Care Resource and Referral Agencies (NACCRRA). This is the umbrella organization your local Resource and Referral agency belongs to. Besides providing you with referrals from parents, they are a clearinghouse of educational material and information. They sponsor and advertise local child care events (fairs, exhibits, workshops) in which you can participate and promote your business. They can provide you with referrals for insurance companies, food program sponsors, and other services you might need. R & R's commonly serve as a job bank for individuals looking for employment in child care as well. And they routinely sponsor trainings and workshops for providers. Your R & R is a friend indeed. You will be put in touch with your local agency as you go through the licensing process. For those who are not required to be licensed or registered, phone the NACCRRA headquarters (see the Appendix) for a referral to your closest R & R.

Local organizations are also available to you as a source of workshops, networking, and training. Your local food program sponsor, state and county department of education, vocational institute, YWCA, and community college or university all offer periodic classes and training for those who live and/or work with young children. Subscribing to your local parenting newsletter or magazine (for example, *Seattle's Child* or *LA Parent*) will often gain you generous mailings of flyers and circulars advertising classes and workshops. The wider your network, the more opportunities will become available to you.

All of the above suggestions will help you become a part of the wider early childhood network. Nothing, however, can substitute for the support and information you receive by having your own informal provider support group. Most providers knew an experienced provider before they opened their own family child care. Networking and keeping in touch with this person is a good way to start your own informal group. Soon, these informal groups grow and you find yourselves meeting once every month or so for tea and sympathy, and of course, exchange of information. The old adage "There's power in numbers" is true; a problem you've been struggling with will benefit from having two or three extra minds considering it.

In addition, it's always nice to have a provider or two nearby with whom you can share parent/child referrals. If you're up to capacity and get an inquiry, you can refer the parent to your provider friend. She can do the same for you. In addition, some providers "share" a part-time child (he's at one child care Monday, Wednesday, and Thursday, and at another on Tuesday and Friday).

Planning for Accreditation

As you become experienced at providing family child care, you may wish to apply for accreditation through NAFCC. The purpose of accreditation is to give professional recognition and an opportunity to heighten parents' awareness of the high quality of the provider's child care.

This is the way it works. After you have been a family child care provider for eighteen months and are duly licensed or registered in your state, you are eligible to apply for accreditation from NAFCC. It is a process that involves self-evaluation and then outside review, observation, and evaluation by a child care professional (NAFCC calls them "Validators") and an independent parent.

The following seven dimensions of child care are scrutinized:

- *Indoor safety.* This includes the bathroom and diaper changing area, kitchen, sleeping area, "indoor physical space" (play area and objects), and transportation safety.
- *Health.* This includes personal hygiene (provider's and children's), basic health care (identifying illnesses, injuries, sexual or physical abuse, and appropriate provider response), first aid, and healthy maintenance of pets.
- *Nutrition.* This includes serving balanced, nutritious meals, using a food service that meets children's individual needs, and the serving of food in a positive, relaxed, social atmosphere.
- *Learning Environment.* The validator looks for a learning environment that facilitates the differing developmental needs of children, offers exploratory play, fosters a sense of

belonging, and includes a variety of developmentally appropriate toys and books.

The toys and books looked at include manipulative materials (flexible toys with moveable parts), language materials, music materials, self-help materials (for example, child-size housekeeping toys), art materials, dramatic play materials (dolls, cars, costumes), life-skills objects (kitchen utensils, safe tools, computers), and large-muscle materials (ride-on toys, balls, slides).

In addition, the validator looks for a balance of activities (independent play and guided activities), multicultural awareness, a supportive schedule or structure, and encouragement of children's independence.

- *Interacting.* This dimension addresses the relationship between the provider and the children—checking for a warm and nurturing way of relating, appropriate communication techniques, positive guidance, and a general attentive and responsive attitude toward the children.
- *Outdoor play environment.* Checkpoints here are health and safety, a variety of play and learning experiences, and particular attention paid to water hazards.
- *Professional responsibility.* The validator checks for comprehensive, written policies, complete, current child records, structure of communication with parents, ongoing provider education, compliance with state regulations, and clear policies and procedures for assistants.

Providers report that going through the accreditation process is a real learning experience and self-esteem booster. You find out what you're already doing right and become very focused on ways to improve your business. Standards for accreditation are higher than most state licensing regulations, so providers who become accredited feel very confident about citing their accreditation to parents as a unique feature of their business (and in states where there are no regulations, accreditation will make your daycare a real stand-out). Recognition and certification from a national organization also boosts your image as a professional; it reinforces the fact that being a family child care provider takes special skills—not just anyone can do it. Lastly, the accreditation process gets you energized and excited about the quality and potential of your child care business and keeps the job challenging.

When you are ready, contact NAFCC for the accreditation application forms, study guide, and fees.

Setting Goals

Making goals, reviewing your progress toward the goals, and reaching them is an integral part of any business. Highly successful people set goals and monitor their own progress on a regular basis. Here are three components of setting goals.

- The goal must be specific. "I will keep good records" is too vague. You must state exactly and specifically what you will do. For example, "I will keep accurate and organized attendance records."
- The goal must be measurable. A measurable form of the above goal would be, "I will keep accurate and organized attendance records each month." At the end of the month, you can look and see if you have indeed kept accurate and organized attendance records.
- The goal must have a deadline. Studies have found that we achieve our goals far more consistently if we have a deadline to meet. So the goal above could further be restated, "I will keep accurate and organized attendance records to be completed by the last day of each month."

The following are some thoughts on where you might be in one, three, and five years from now, and some sample goals set by individual providers.

One Year

At the end of their first year in business, most providers are just catching their breath. This is a good time to take a day to sit back, look over the events of the year, evaluate your performance or success in specific areas, and set goals for the future.

As a general guide, evaluate yourself in the following areas:

1. Record keeping—Am I maintaining accurate, timely, and well-organized records?
   Meals (CACFP records)
   Attendance
   Income
   Expenses
2. Daily activities
   Schedule—Is it working reasonably well for the children? For me? For the parents?
   Activities—Do I have an appropriate mix of free play and structured activities?
3. Environment
   Does my facility adequately meet the needs of my business? What changes might improve it?
   Safety—Are there concerns that have come up over the past year? How have I addressed them?
4. Relationships
   Are my policies clear to the parents and children? Are they signed by each and every parent?
   Are there children/parents who need to be terminated?
   How is my family reacting to and coping with the business?
5. Business
   Have I made a profit? If not, where am I over-budget?
   How did my marketing tools for generating enrollment work?
   Which ones will I discard or use again?

This list of questions should help you pinpoint areas that need work. Once you have identified trouble spots, you can include them in your goal-setting.

The following are typical provider goals for the first year in business.

- By the end of the year I will have turned a profit.
- By year's end, I will have a preschool curriculum program

developed and in use.
- By year's end, I will have organized, easily-accessed records on business expenses for tax purposes.

Three Years

After two to three years in family day care, most providers who are not suited to the business have gotten out and those remaining have developed a stable child care program and a solvent business for themselves. This is a common time for many providers to expand to a large license and really make a financial success of family child care. The section earlier in this chapter about staying small or expanding to a large license describes some of the benefits and trade-offs of such growth.

Regardless of whether you expand or not, this is a good time for you to take another look at your skills and background and determine if there are still holes you need to fill. Some questions to ask yourself are:

1. Am I up-to-date on infant and child first aid and CPR?
2. Which curriculum areas in my program are tired and could use some new ideas?
3. Would a class or seminar on parent-provider relations be of use to me at this point?
4. (If you have assistants) Is there a class on managing others that would be useful for me to take?
5. Is it possible for me to attend the next national conference of NAFCC or NAEYC?

The following are common goals for providers after two to three years in business.

- At the end of three years, I will have taken four courses in the areas of parent involvement, curriculum, and safety.
- At the end of three years, I will be earning enough money after expenses and taxes to pay for 50 percent of my daughter's yearly college tuition.
- At the end of three years, I will upgrade to a large license.

Five Years

The providers who have reached the five-year mark are truly professionals in early childhood care. Their program is solid and their business is very stable and generally quite profitable. Looking ahead to where you want to be in five years, think long-term. Be ambitious in your goal-setting and tune in to the dreams you have for your career as a whole. It's never too early to set goals, but five years is a long time in the future to think about specific program questions.

- At the end of five years in business, I will have completed my early childhood education degree.
- At the end of five years, my partner and I will take the first steps toward opening up a commercial child care center.
- At the end of five years, I will turn the garage into an extra room.

Don't neglect to do this kind of long-term thinking even if planning daily menus and activities is more fun; the more time you spend in business planning now, the smoother the growth of your business will be.

A Word about Professionalism

Unfortunately, when it comes to planning, you must also expect to encounter a certain amount of ignorance and lack of respect for your profession and decide how you will deal with it. You've already heard from other providers that parents will not shower you with appreciation and respect for the good job you do. In general, that is true of our society as a whole; people who work with children, especially young children, are viewed as paid babysitters rather than professionals. Sadly, this attitude is even more prevalent when you work in your home.

Combatting this perception begins with you. The resounding advice from successful, experienced providers is: *Develop an attitude*. Insist on respect for the vitally important service you provide. Deborah, an experienced provider, shares her thoughts on this.

> I wish someone had told me about the lack of respect. I'd worked in early childhood in center settings before I had children—but I really felt the disrespect when I opened my own business in my home. I felt it from parents, other professionals, and even from some of my own family child care colleagues who don't respect themselves. I found I had to take charge and demand the respect I deserved.

The language you use is important. Be sure to refer to your business in professional terms. For example, notice the difference in the following statements:

> *You say to your husband, "after a day of watching the kids, I'm exhausted." Or,*
> *"A full day of child care takes a lot of energy."*
> *You say to the life insurance representative, "Tuesday isn't good for me—the children are here." Or,*
> *"I work on Tuesdays."*

Which comments sound like a babysitter's? Which ones sound like the statements of a professional? Be careful of how you label yourself. People will take their cue from you. If you have a healthy respect for your career and are not shy about saying so, it will encourage others to respect your career as well.

Lisa talks about self-respect:

> I was raised to be very modest and not blow my own horn. I do consider myself successful, but was hesitant to say anything that might be construed as bragging. My husband helped me change what I thought was bragging into healthy respect. In groups, he would refer to "Lisa's business" in little ways that would open conversations and clearly show that my business was every bit as important to our family as his job in management. In time, I learned to speak just as confidently.

Susan points out that how you operate your business also gives others important cues as to how you want to be perceived.

Be as professional as possible. Do what you say you will do:

Bill the parents, charge late fees, enforce your policies. You own a business—run it like one.

In today's society, there really is no place for any kind of discounting of the importance of child care. Our children and their care are too critical to discount, belittle, undermine, or overlook. So get your attitude in order and communicate clearly to the world that family child care is your profession and a vital one at that.

A Wish for Success

Working with young children is not easy, but it is immensely rewarding. As you embark on your business venture and become embroiled in preparations and planning, don't forget to enjoy yourself. Caring for children is an important job and you are to be congratulated for your choice. One provider described her job this way, "I'm in the business of socializing the next generation."

I wish you good luck and much success.

Appendix

Publications

Books on Food/Meals

Baxter, Kathleen. *Come & Get It: A Natural Foods Cookbook for Children.* Ann Arbor, MI: Children's First Press, 1978.

Dunkle, Jac Lynn, and Martha Shore Edwards. *The (No Leftovers!) Child Care Cookbook.* St. Paul: Redleaf Press, 1992.

Warren, Jean. *Super Snacks: Seasonal Sugarless Snacks.* Everett, WA: Warren Publishing, 1992.

Business Books

Copeland, Tom. *Basic Guide to Family Child Care Record Keeping, 4th ed.* St. Paul: Redleaf Press, 1992.

Copeland, Tom. *Family Child Care Tax Workbook.* St. Paul: Redleaf Press, 1992. (Updated every year.)

Nelson, Eileen, ed. *Calendar-Keeper.* St. Paul: Redleaf Press. (New edition each year.)

Newsletters and Journals

Family Child Caring, Redleaf Press, six issues per year.

Super Snack News: Nutritious Foods, Facts and Fun from Totline Publications, Warren Publishing, twelve issues per year.

Totline Newsletter: Activity Newsletter for Working with Young Children, Warren Publishing, six issues per year.

Books on Activities to Do with Children

Bittinger, Gayle. *Exploring Sand and the Desert.* Everett, WA: Warren Publishing, 1993.

Bittinger, Gayle. *Exploring Water and the Ocean.* Everett, WA: Warren Publishing, 1993.

Bittinger, Gayle. *1, 2, 3 Science*. Everett, WA: Warren Publishing, 1993.

Bittinger, Gayle. *Our Selves*. Everett, WA: Warren Publishing, 1992.

Bittinger, Gayle. *Our World*. Everett, WA: Warren Publishing, 1990.

Bos, Bev. *Before the Basics: Creating Conversations with Children*. Roseville, CA: Turn the Page Press, 1983.

Haas, Carolyn Buhai. *Look at Me: Activities for Babies and Toddlers*. Chicago: Chicago Review Press, 1985.

Colgin, Mary Lou. *One Potato, Two Potato: Chants for Children*. Mt. Rainier, MD: Gryphon House, 1982.

Connolly, Anne Marie, and Helen Gibson. *Rainy Day Activities for Preschoolers*. Mercer Island, WA: Mercer Island Preschool Association, 1988.

Gesme, Carole. *Ups and Downs with Feelings: A Game for Ages 3–6*. Minnetonka, MN: Carole Gesme, Inc., 1987.

Hendrickson, Karen. *Baby and I Can Play & Fun with Toddlers*. Seattle: Parenting Press, 1990.

Kohl, Mary Ann. *Good Earth Art: Environmental Art for Kids*. Bellingham, WA: Bright Ring Publishing, 1991.

Kohl, Mary Ann. *Mudworks: Creative Clay, Dough, and Modeling Experiences*. Bellingham, WA: Bright Ring Publishing, 1989.

Kohl, Mary Ann. *Scribble Cookies and Other Independent Creative Art Experiences for Children*. Bellingham, WA: Bright Ring Publishing, 1986.

McKinnon, Elizabeth. *Special Day Celebrations*. Everett, WA: Warren Publishing, 1989.

Miller, Karen. *Things to Do with Toddlers and Twos*. Chelsea, MA: Telshare Publishing, 1984.

Silberg, Jackie. *Games to Play with Babies*. Mt. Rainier, MD: Gryphon House, 1993.

Silberg, Jackie. *Games to Play with Toddlers*. Mt. Rainier, MD: Gryphon House, 1993.

Steelsmith, Shari. *Peekaboo and Other Games to Play with Your Baby*. Seattle: Parenting Press, 1994.

Warren, Jean. *1, 2, 3 Art*. Everett, WA: Warren Publishing, 1985.

Warren, Jean. *1, 2, 3 Colors*. Everett, WA: Warren Publishing, 1988.

Warren, Jean. *1, 2, 3 Math*. Everett, WA: Warren Publishing, 1992.

Warren, Jean. *Piggyback Songs*. Everett, WA: Warren Publishing, 1984.

Warren, Jean. *Theme-A-Saurus*. Everett, WA: Warren Publishing, 1989.

Warren, Jean. *Toddler Theme-A-Saurus*. Everett, WA: Warren Publishing, 1991.

Books on Children's Safety

Boelts, Maribeth and Darwin. *Kids to the Rescue! First Aid Techniques for Kids*. Seattle: Parenting Press, 1992.

Buschman, Janis, and Debbie Hunley. *Strangers Don't Look Like the Big Bad Wolf*. Edmonds, WA: Chas. Franklin Press, 1985.

Fleisher, Gary R. *Barron's First Aid for Kids*. Hauppage, New York: Barrons Educational Series, 1987.

Freeman, Lory. *It's MY Body*. Seattle: Parenting Press, 1983.

Freeman, Lory. *Loving Touches*. Seattle: Parenting Press, 1986.

Green, Martin. *A Sigh of Relief: The First Aid Handbook for Childhood Emergencies*. New York: Bantam Books, 1979.

Johnsen, Karen. *The Trouble with Secrets*. Seattle: Parenting Press, 1986.

Books on Guidance

Ames, Louise Bates, et al. Books from the Gesell Institute of Human Development. New York: Bantam, Doubleday, Dell.
Your One-Year-Old
Your Two-Year-Old
Your Three-Year-Old
Your Four-Year-Old
Your Five-Year-Old
Briggs, Dorothy Corkille. *Your Child's Self-Esteem*. New York: Doubleday, 1970.

Clarke, Jean Illsley. *Developmental Affirmations*. Plymouth, MN: Daisy Press, 1986.

Clarke, Jean Illsley, and Connie Dawson. *Growing Up Again*. New York: HarperCollins, 1989.

Clarke, Jean Illsley. *Self-Esteem: A Family Affair*. New York: Harper & Row, 1978.

Crary, Elizabeth. *Kids Can Cooperate*. Seattle: Parenting Press, 1984.

Crary, Elizabeth. *Magic Tools for Raising Kids*. Seattle: Parenting Press, 1994.

Crary, Elizabeth. *Pick Up Your Socks*. Seattle: Parenting Press, 1990.

Crary, Elizabeth. *365 Wonderful, Wacky, Ways to Get Your Children to Do What You Want*. Seattle: Parenting Press, 1994.

Crary, Elizabeth. *Without Spanking or Spoiling*. Seattle: Parenting Press, 1993.

Eyre, Richard and Linda. *Teaching Your Children Values*. New York: Simon & Schuster, 1993.

Faber, Adele, and Elaine Mazlish. *How to Talk So Kids Will Listen and Listen So Kids Will Talk*. New York: Avon Books, 1980.

Samalin, Nancy, and Catherine Whitney. *Love and Anger*. New York: Penguin Books, 1991.

Van der Zande, Irene. *1, 2, 3 . . . The Toddler Years*. Santa Cruz, CA: Santa Cruz Toddler Care Center, 1990.

Whitham, Cynthia. *Win the Whining War*. Los Angeles: Perspective Publishing, 1991.

Stories and Other Books for Children

There are literally thousands of children's books available. Here are just a few tried-and-true favorites. Ask your librarian or bookseller to suggest more.

For Babies

Cohen, Marsha. *Baby's Favorite Things*. New York: Random House, 1986.

Hoban, Tana. *1, 2, 3: A First Book of Numbers*. New York: Greenwillow Books, 1986.

Hoban, Tana. *Red, Blue, Yellow Shoe: A First Book of Colors*. New York: Greenwillow Books, 1986.

Hoban, Tana. *What Is It? A First Book of Objects*. New York: Greenwillow Books, 1985.

Kunhardt, Dorothy. *Pat the Bunny*. Racine, WI: Western Publishing Co. 1992.

Maccarone, Grace. *Baby's Toys*. New York: Scholastic/Avon, 1990.

Oxenbury, Helen. *All Fall Down*. New York: Aladdin Books/Macmillan, 1987.

Oxenbury, Helen. *Clap Hands*. New York: Aladdin Books/Macmillan, 1987.

Oxenbury, Helen. *Goodnight, Good Morning*. New York: Dial Books, 1982.

Oxenbury, Helen. *Say Goodnight*. New York: Aladdin Books/Macmillan, 1987.

Oxenbury, Helen. *Tickle, Tickle*. New York: Aladdin Books/Macmillan, 1987.

Wells, Rosemary. *Max's Bath*. New York: Dial Books, 1985.

Wells, Rosemary. *Max's Bedtime*. New York: Dial Books, 1985.

For Toddlers

Ahlberg, Janet and Allan. *Each Peach, Pear, Plum*. New York: Puffin Books, 1978.

Asch, Frank. *Just Like Daddy*. New York: Simon & Schuster, 1981.

Brown, Margaret Wise. *Goodnight Moon*. New York: Harper Collins, 1947.

Brown, Margaret Wise. *Runaway Bunny*. New York: Harper Collins, 1942.

Brown, Ruth. *A Dark, Dark Tale*. New York: Dial Books, 1981.

Carle, Eric. *The Very Hungry Caterpillar*. New York: Philomel Books, 1987.

Carle, Eric. *The Very Quiet Cricket*. New York: Philomel Books, 1990.

de Angeli, Marguerite. *Book of Nursery and Mother Goose Rhymes*. New York: Doubleday, 1954.

Hennessy, B. G. *Jake Baked the Cake*. New York: Puffin Books, 1990.

Oxenbury, Helen. *We're Going on a Bear Hunt*. New York: Macmillan, 1989.

Pallotta, Jerry. *The Yucky Reptile Alphabet Book*. Watertown, MA: Charlesbridge Publishing, 1989.

Shaw, Nancy. *Sheep in a Jeep*. Boston: Houghton Mifflin, 1986.

Wells, Rosemary. *Max's Dragon Shirt*. New York: Dial Books, 1991.

For Preschoolers

Bemelmans, Ludwig. *Madeline*. New York: Puffin Books, 1977.

Bingham, Mindy. *Minou*. Santa Barbara, CA: Advocacy Press, 1987.

Brett, Jan. *The Trouble with Trolls*. Putnam, New York: 1993.

Burleigh, Robert. *Flight: The Journey of Charles Lindbergh*. New York: Philomel Books, 1991.

Carroll, Lewis. *Jabberwocky* (illustrated by Graeme Base). New York: Simon & Schuster, 1987.

Crary, Elizabeth. The Children's Problem Solving Series. Seattle: Parenting Press.
I Want It
I Can't Wait
I Want to Play
My Name Is Not Dummy
I'm Lost
Mommy, Don't Go

Greenfield, Eloise. *Honey, I Love: And Other Love Poems*. New York: Harper Trophy, 1986.

Kirby, David, and Allen Woodman. *The Cows Are Going to Paris*. Honesdale, PA: Boyd Mills Press, 1991.

Leaf, Munro. *The Story of Ferdinand*. New York: Puffin Books, 1936.

Mayer, Mercer. *There's a Nightmare in My Closet*. New York: Dell, 1968.

Meyer, Linda. *Harriet Tubman: They Called Me Moses*. Seattle: Parenting Press, 1988.

Rey, H. A. *Curious George*. Boston: Houghton Mifflin, 1941.

Sendak, Maurice. *Where the Wild Things Are*. New York: HarperCollins, 1963.

Steelsmith, Shari. *Elizabeth Blackwell: Story of the First Woman Doctor*. Seattle: Parenting Press, 1987.

Steelsmith, Shari. *Juliette Gordon Low: Founder of the Girl Scouts*. Seattle: Parenting Press, 1990.

Wells, Rosemary. *Voyage to the Bunny Planet Series: First Tomato; Moss Pillows; The Island Light*. New York: Dial Books, 1992.

Music/Tapes for Young Children

As with books, there are hundreds of recordings of children's music available. Here are only eight suggestions, but it is a place to start. See your children's bookseller for more suggestions.

Bartels, Joanie. *Morningtime Magic*. Discovery Music.

Bartels, Joanie. *Sillytime Magic*. Discovery Music.

Berman, Marcia. *Rabbits Dance and Other Songs*. Learning Through Movement.

Hunter, Tom. *Windows*. The Song Growing Company.

Hysom, Dennis. *Dennis Hysom Sings the Wooley Cat's Favorite Nursery Rhymes*. Discovery Music.

Lafond, Lois. *I Am Who I Am*. Lois Lafond & Co.

Miss Jackie. *Sniggles, Squirrels and Chicken Pox*. Miss Jackie Music Co.

Prokofiev, Serge. *Peter and the Wolf: A Musical Tale for Children*. Philips Classics.

Raffi. *Singable Songs for the Very Young*. MCA Records.

Mail-order catalogs where many of these publications and products can be found

Children's Small Press Collection
719 North 4th Ave.
Ann Arbor, MI 48104
(800) 668–8056

Creative Parenting Catalog
P.O. Box 75267
Seattle, WA 98125
(800) 992–6657

Lakeshore Curriculum Materials Company
2695 East Dominguez St.
Carson, CA 90749
(310) 537–8600

Redleaf Press Catalog
450 North Syndicate, Suite 5
St. Paul, MN 55104
(800) 423–8309

Totline Resource Catalog
P.O. Box 2250
Everett, WA 98203
(800) 334–4769

Software

Business Programs

CashPro. Striata, Inc. P.O. Box 4747, Salem, OR.
Quicken and *Quick Book*. Intuit, 66 Willow Place, Menlo Park,
    CA 94025. (Available in stores.)
Word. Microsoft Corp., One Microsoft Way, Redmond, WA
    98052. (Available in stores.)

WordPerfect. WordPerfect Corp., 1555 North Technology Way, Orem, UT 84057. (Available in stores.)

Child Care Management Systems

Child Care 2000, operates on IBM/DOS, single user or network system. Care Software Systems, Inc., P.O. Box 1530, Dublin, OH 43017.

ChildPlus III, operates on IBM/DOS. Management Information Technology USA, 800–888–6674.

EZ-Care, operates on IBM/DOS. Softerware, Inc., 540 Pennsylvania Ave., Fort Washington, PA 19034. This is the leading system for center management.

Maggey, operates on IBM/DOS. Childcare Management Services, Inc., 299 South Park Ave., #2, Tucson, AZ 85719.

MacCare, operates on Macintosh. Softerware, Inc., 540 Pennsylvania Ave., Fort Washington, PA 19034.

Private Advantage, operates on Macintosh. Mt. Taylor Programs, 716 College Avenue, #D, Santa Rosa, CA 95404.

Professional Organizations

National Association for Family Child Care (NAFCC)
1331-A Pennsylvania Ave. NW, Suite 348
Washington, DC 20004
(800) 359–3817

National Association for the Education of Young Children (NAEYC)
1834 Connecticut Ave. NW
Washington, DC 20009
(800) 424–2460

National Association of Child Care Resource and Referral Agencies (NACCRRA)
2116 Campus Drive SE
Rochester, MN 55904
507–287–2220

Index

About the Author

Shari Steelsmith is a freelance writer and editor specializing in topics on family and early childhood education. She is also the author of *Peekaboo—and Other Games to Play with Your Baby* and two biographies for children. Ms. Steelsmith lives and works in Hemet, California, with her husband, infant son, and cat. She is currently at work on a book about children and anger.